D0764610

THE
LEADERBOARD

THE

LEADER

CONVERSATIONS

BOARD

ON GOLF AND LIFE

Amy Alcott with Don Wade

ATRIA BOOKS

New York • London • Toronto • Sydney

ATRIA BOOKS

A Division of Simon & Schuster, Inc.
1230 Avenue of the Americas
New York, NY 10020

First Atria Books hardcover edition March 2009

ATRIA BOOKS and colophon are trademarks of Simon & Schuster, Inc.

For information about special discounts for bulk purchases,
please contact Simon & Schuster Special Sales at
1-800-456-6798 or business@simonandschuster.com.

The Simon & Schuster Speakers Bureau can bring authors to your
live event. For more information or to book an event, contact the
Simon & Schuster Speakers Bureau at 866-248-3049 or visit our
website at www.simonspeakers.com.

Designed by Dana Sloan

Manufactured in the United States of America

10 9 8 7 6 5 4 3 2

Library of Congress Cataloging-in-Publication Data

Alcott, Amy.
  The leaderboard : conversations on golf and life / Amy Alcott.
    p. cm.
  1. Golf—Anecdotes. 2. Golf—Interviews. I. Title.

GV967.A43 2009
796.352—dc22

                                                2008053568

ISBN-13: 978-1-4165-3542-3
ISBN-10:   1-4165-3542-X

To my wonderful parents, Lea and Eugene, who, in their own styles, gave me unconditional love and a strong foundation to navigate this world. Thanks for raising me in a home with Mantovani, tennis rackets, jai alai cestas, Modigliani prints, eclectic conversation, and manners, and for instilling a love of animals and an understanding of the importance of giving. Your lessons were the fuel for my life, and I still rely on them.

Lastly, thank you for the cut-down club with the magenta shaft and black electrical-tape grip.

CONTENTS

FOREWORD

by Jim Nantz

ORMALLY, WHEN INTERACTING with a star as accomplished as Amy Alcott, most people tend to want to know everything about *her*. So it's something quite out of the ordinary to find a living legend who more often than not will initiate a conversation with a relaxed smile and a gleam in her eye that suggests, "Hey, I want to know more about *you*!"

This rare ability to not take herself so seriously, coupled with her knack for making people around her feel comfortable, is why Amy makes friends as easily as she makes birdies.

What's truly remarkable is the eclectic nature of the people who populate her world—as is evident by the cross-section of society that she has interviewed for this book. Amy seems to "collect friends" the way Warren Buffett amasses stocks— with an emphasis on underlying value and growth potential. For example, my CBS colleague Steve Kroft and former president Bill Clinton may hold divergent views about how certain news stories ought to be covered, but they clearly share their love of golf—and friendships with Amy.

It's easy to understand why creative people—athletes, artists, executives, etc.—are naturally attracted to her. She's a smart, self-confident, and relentlessly curious woman who'd be a winner at almost any endeavor she might have chosen to pursue. Above all, it's great *fun* to be in Amy's company. You just never know where her passion might express itself next. Remember, this is the woman who pioneered what has become the champion's ritual victory jump into the pond adjoining the eighteenth green at Mission Hills. She revels in surprise and spontaneity.

In its own way, executing her vision for this book also involved "taking a plunge" of sorts. But then again, whether it's on the course or in her post-competitive career, Amy Alcott has never been the sort to lay up or take a gimme. Rather, she has always done things her way—trusting her instincts, taking calculated risks, and finding new angles.

To be sure, she is not the first author to compile celebrity interviews about lessons learned on the fairways and greens that carry over into the boardroom or onto the stage and screen. In the traditional literary formula, Amy herself would serve as the primary focus of the interview, and the accumulated wisdom and knowledge that she dispenses would drive the narrative. But here, in what I believe truly *is* a first, it's the hall of famer who turns the tables and does the *asking*, not the answering; the *listening*, not the talking; and the *learning*, not the instructing.

As a golf book, this one is a typically daring Amy Alcott aim-for-the-flag shot. There are plenty of menacing hazards guarding the green: Would the interviews turn out to be enlightening? What could *amateurs*—such as a famous composer, a former tennis champion, or a basketball immortal—teach about golf? And for that matter, what can former golf champions teach about life?

This isn't a novel, so technically there is no ending to give away. But that doesn't mean that there isn't a special payoff awaiting those who complete the book. I won't spoil the surprise, but I will say this: If you thought that Amy could impart spin and make a golf ball do all sorts of tricks, just wait until you get hooked into this book—and you will, because, let's face it, everyone fantasizes about being able to be that proverbial "fly on the wall" who can eavesdrop on the rich and famous. To her credit, Amy has redefined the standard Q&A genre; what she does instead is to invite you to pull up a chair and join her as she holds court in a virtual clubhouse *schmooze*-fest.

The responses to Amy's well-chosen questions contain important pieces of a larger puzzle. When fitted together, they form a meaningful mosaic that is far larger and more illuminating—just as the whole of every great golf course is greater than the sum of its holes. Here, what appear to be random reflections scattered throughout the pages of this volume ultimately coalesce into one powerful mirror that shines a penetrating light right back upon the reader. You may *think* you're reading about celebrities, but all the while you're really learning more about *yourself*.

Like Amy herself, *The Leaderboard* is thoughtful, provocative, and fun. I'll bet that it, too, will create quite a splash.

PREFACE

Aፑᴛᴇʀ ᴘʟᴀʏɪɴɢ ɢᴏʟꜰ for forty-one years, I've had a great time writing this book.

When I told people about the book, most assumed I would write an autobiography since I've had so many rich experiences playing golf around the globe. But I chose to take a different path. While the book is about golf, it really is more about the wonderful people I've encountered.

Playing tournament golf opened many doors for me, but it is the people I've met, and the stories they've shared with me on the fairways and greens we've walked, that I find so rewarding. They truly are a remarkable cast of characters who come from all walks of life. Let's face it—as my mom, Lea, used to say—life is a people business.

Some of those people included here are fellow players, such as Jane Blalock, Dottie Pepper, Annika Sorenstam, Karrie Webb, Ben Crenshaw, Ken Venturi, and one of my new personal favorites, Lorena Ochoa. Others are show-business people I met when I was growing up and living in Los Angeles. How would you like to be able to count Jack Nicholson, Kenny G., and Les Moonves as friends? And how about former president Bill Clinton? I probably couldn't, if it hadn't been for golf.

I'm struck by the names of those I would like to have interviewed had they still been alive. Dinah Shore is high on that list because she was a very special person to me, both personally and for what she meant to the LPGA. And I would love to have interviewed two of my all-time favorite golfers, Babe Zaharias and Patty Berg. Jack Lemmon and I talked about golf quite a bit, but sadly he died before I wrote this book.

As much as I have enjoyed these relationships and becoming a public figure, there's a part of me that is very private—at times, almost reclusive. While I can be the life of the party, I'm also given to deep introspection. Both sides of my personality served me well as a competitor, but throughout my career, my private side could result in a sense of loneliness. As an athlete, I needed to be myopic. That is something I share with all athletes who strive to be the best they can be. Golf was my constant companion. It helped carry me through difficult times and kept me balanced.

Yet, in my heart of hearts, I've always been a people person. I learned the value of giving of oneself and making others feel special from my mother, who taught by example. That will always be her number one Life Lesson.

It is this lesson that has inspired me to explore the lives of some of the most fascinating people I've met throughout my career. Their stories center on golf but also deal with how the game they love intersects with their lives. I came away with a deeper appreciation of how, in the end, the lessons of golf are often the lessons of life.

I hope you enjoy sharing their stories and insights as much as I enjoyed hearing them firsthand. As I worked on this book, I kept coming back to one of Nick Nolte's lines at the end of the film *The Prince of Tides*: "It's the mystery of life that sustains me now."

I have the same feeling.

—Amy Alcott

JANE BLALOCK

I'VE KNOWN JANE BLALOCK since I joined the LPGA in 1975. At that time she was one of the biggest stars on our Tour, having been Rookie of the Year in 1969 after a fine amateur career that saw her win the New Hampshire Amateur five times and the New England Amateur in 1968. In the course of her career, she won twenty-seven tournaments, although she never won a major, finishing second in the LPGA Championship twice. In 1972, she won the inaugural Colgate Dinah Shore Winner's Circle, which later was designated as a major. One of the most consistent players in LPGA history, Jane made 299 straight cuts from 1969 until 1980.

In 1972, the LPGA's Executive Board, reacting to accusations from players, charged Jane with cheating, claiming that she mismarked her ball on the green. Twenty-nine LPGA players signed a petition calling for her suspension, and the Executive Committee ultimately suspended her for one year. Jane sued and won a temporary injunction that allowed her to continue playing. She went on to lead the Tour with five wins that year, despite the incredible pressure she was under. Eventually, the courts found the LPGA in violation of antitrust laws.

After winning twice in 1985, Jane retired from active competition, became a stockbroker, and started a golf management company. Her company started the LPGA Golf Clinics for Women program, and she played a key role in establishing the Legends Tour for LPGA players ages forty-five and older.

We visited at the World Golf Village during the 2007 Handa Cup, a Legends Tour competition between the United States and an international team. I'm happy to report that our team won. We began by talking about her decision to retire after the 1985 season.

. . .

Coming into the 1985 season, I had gone three years without a victory, which was very hard to take. I didn't want to just be out there to play if I wasn't able to win. But earlier in the year I won the Kemper Open at Kaanapali, and then I won the Mazda in Japan. I shot a 64 on a legitimate par-73 course, which was my career low round. At the awards ceremony, I thought, *It just doesn't get any better than this.* But I also recall the feeling that my competitive desire was slipping away. I made a conscious decision at that point that I was going to retire. I wanted to go out with a win.

Was it like a spiritual awakening, an epiphany?

It was somewhat spiritual, I guess. I just really knew it was time. I've never regretted the decision.

Is that when you started your company?

No. Over the years I had made friends with a lot of people in the investment world, and the people at Merrill Lynch in Boston had told me that if I ever wanted to work as a stockbroker, they'd have a job for me. I started on the retail side and then moved over to institutional sales. I enjoyed it and was a stockbroker for five years. In that time, I played in a lot of local charitable events and outings, and I just thought they could be produced better. Also, back then more women were entering the workforce, so it seemed like a good opportunity. We started with four or five very good clients, but it really took off when I convinced Jan Thompson at Mazda to sponsor the LPGA Golf Clinics for Women. The Legends Tour came after that.

How has golf influenced your life?

There are a few ways. First, I never gave up on the golf course. I made 299 cuts, which I'm very proud of. If I shot an 80 in the first round, I wouldn't allow myself to give up. I felt that if you gave up once, you could give up at any time. Golf taught me perseverance. That's what enabled me to win. I'm the same way in business. If someone tells me an idea can never work, it just adds fuel to the fire. It makes me all the more determined to make it work. Second, golf taught me the importance of planning. You can't just show up and expect to play well. You have to have worked on every aspect of your game. In business, you have to have all the answers for any question you might be asked. Finally, you must be able to adapt as conditions change. That's true in golf, in business, and in life.

Was reinventing yourself as a businessperson scary?

It was exhilarating. I knew golf so well, but going to Merrill Lynch was a completely new world. I was forty years old and moving to a new city. I had to get a whole new wardrobe and make a new set of friends. But I needed new challenges. I needed to get out of my comfort zone. And your status changes because you're no longer recognized as a star golfer. It's kind of a shock when you realize that people don't know who you are or what you did in your former life. You have to deal with developing a whole new persona.

Are there any people you'd like to spend time with, not necessarily on the golf course but just to get to know?

Mikhail Baryshnikov would be the first name that comes to mind. He's the greatest male ballet dancer and I think probably the ultimate athlete. He was just beautiful to watch. The second person would be Helen Turley, who has been at the center of the American winemaking industry. She's been very successful in a field that has traditionally been dominated by men. I'm a wine collector, so I'd love to just sit down with her and try some of her favorite wines and listen to her explain why they're so special.

What was your most exciting moment on the golf course?

I have three, and they're all equally special. The first was winning the Triple Crown at Mission Hills. I beat Judy Rankin and Joanne Carner in a playoff. It was the only time my parents saw me win on tour. The second was winning the Kemper in 1985. I had never worked harder and was frustrated. I had come close to retiring a couple of times, so it ended a slump and unlocked the handcuffs. The third was winning my last tournament, because it allowed me to retire on a high note. Winning is a lonely experience, but it's the only reason I ever played. I never cared about the money. Winning was everything.

How did you get through the controversy when you were accused of cheating? That must have been incredibly difficult.

I'm a very resilient, positive person. I believe in always looking at the sun, because that way you never see the shadows. I also had tremendous support from my family and friends and from the press.

How did it change you?

It made me stronger, but it also made me less trusting, which is not a good thing. But it didn't make me a harder person, which could easily have happened. What was scary, besides the charges themselves, was the fact that it snowballed. It dragged on for three or four years. It's interesting that I've received apologies from many of the players who made the charges, admitting they were wrong. I can take some comfort in that.

. . .

Jane's life is proof that golf gives you many tools to reinvent yourself. She was always a great competitor, but she showed a lot of heart when she battled the allegations of cheating, which is about as bad an allegation as a player can face in golf—a sport that prides itself on being a game of honor and sportsmanship. Winning five tournaments in a year when she was under so much scrutiny says a lot about her both as a person and as a player. When I think about Jane, I remember a quote from Winston Churchill: "Never give in, never give in, never, never, never—in nothing great or small, large or petty—never give in except to convictions of honour and sense."

BILL CLINTON

I MET PRESIDENT CLINTON at his New York City office, on 125th Street and Lenox Avenue, in the historic heart of Harlem, just a short distance from the famous Apollo Theater. The room faces south and has beautiful views of Manhattan. The walls are lined with political posters and photographs, and among the photos are images of some of the true legends of jazz, which reflect his lifelong interest in music.

Before we began our interview, he showed me some of the memorabilia that he keeps on a shelf beneath the windows. He has campaign buttons and pins dating back to the earliest years of our country. As we perused the items he had collected over the years, he was like a youngster showing off his collection of toy cars. I was reminded of just how enthusiastic he is, whether he is talking about golf, history, politics, or the fascinating people he's known over his remarkable career.

In an interview with *Sports Illustrated* many years ago, President Clinton said I was one of his favorite golf partners and mentioned that when we played at Hillcrest, a club in Los Angeles, I shot a 29 on the front nine. A friend asked me if I had actually shot a 29 or if it was what we call a "newspaper score." I have to confess, the president did give me four putts of about eight feet. I tell this story only because people always talk about how President Clinton likes to take mulligans, or, in his case, "Billigans." I think it's because he genuinely likes to see people do well and succeed. That, and his remarkable enthusiasm, are two reasons why many people believe he's the greatest politician of his generation.

I think we connected because during the first round we ever played, we spoke about his relationship with his mother, who had recently died. I was very close to my own mother, and I could relate to the emotions he talked about. I think we forged a sense of intimacy. Oh—and that we also loved the film *Happy, Texas.*

We have played together three times, twice at Hillcrest and once at Riviera, so we began by talking about the state of his golf game.

. . .

It's getting better. I didn't play that much once I left the White House. I spent most of 2003 writing my book, and then in 2004 I had heart surgery and I couldn't play for about six months. When I did start to play again, I had lost some of my touch around the greens but what I really lost is distance. I used to be quite a long hitter, but since the surgery my balance isn't what it used to be. I'm still a good short- to middle-iron player, but I wasn't as good with my long irons. Fortunately, rescue clubs have saved me. Now my big problem is finding time to play. I'm traveling so much for my foundation that when I do get to play, I'm usually jet-lagged or exhausted.

How long have you been playing?

When I was twelve my uncle gave me a set of hickory-shafted clubs, so that's what I learned to play with. I used to caddie from time to time, but back then not many of my friends played golf. I did enter my first tournament when I was sixteen. I remember that it was about one hundred degrees out. A friend of mine who was a really good player caddied for me. I was six or seven down after the first nine, and my friend said he'd do the thinking for us. All I had to do was hit the shots. I came back and was tied after eighteen. I wound up losing on the first hole of the playoff, but every time I see my buddy we have a good laugh about that match. I didn't play for about ten years after high school, and I really kick myself because I was in England as a Rhodes Scholar and could have played all those wonderful courses over there. When I was in my late twenties I started playing with Hillary's brothers, who are golf fanatics. When I was governor I'd work until five or six and then go play at Little Rock Country Club. Right from the beginning, one of the things that really drew me to golf was that it was my way to be alone in nature.

If you had the time to really play and practice, how good could you be?

I'm not sure. Greg Norman once said to me, "If I had you for a month, you'd never shoot higher than the seventies. You don't have a month, do you?"

How much did you get to play as president?

I used to play at the Army Navy Country Club, which isn't far from the White House. It's an old course and not very long, but you've got to really hit shots there. I could just grab someone to play with. I played a lot with Erskine Bowles. He's a very good player. I played with Vernon Jordan and a friend of mine, Kevin O'Keefe, another really good player. I like to play with people who are better than I am.

What about other heads of state?

I'll tell you who is a good player, Jean Chrétien, the former prime minister of Canada. He beat me more than half the times we played. And you know who could be a good player? Tony Blair. One time we were at Chequers, the prime minister's country house. It used to have a golf course but it was sold. We went over and played nine holes. He had never played. I told him I'd drive and we'd both play our second shots from my ball. He parred four of the nine holes. He's just a natural.

Does Hillary play?

She used to play once a year with me, usually when we were on Martha's Vineyard. She played field hockey and was a pretty good tennis player. Once when we were in Bermuda I paid for her to have some lessons, but she just never got into the game. She's one reason I started playing again. She thought I was a workaholic and golf would be good for me. That and singing in the church choir.

Do you have a favorite round of golf?

I love to play links courses. I've never had a good round on one, but I'm just so happy to be there that it doesn't matter. The first time I played Ballybunion in Ireland it was with Christy O'Connor, Senior. About twelve thousand people came out to watch us. The wind was howling. It was a three- or four-club wind. Before we teed off, the caddie asked me what my handicap was. I told him 12. Then he asked if this was the first time I'd played Ballybunion. I told him it was. He said the bet was twenty to one that I wouldn't break 100.

I told him I'd take a piece of that. I made a triple bogey on the first hole. I made a 10 on the second hole, so I'm 9 over par after two holes. I tripled the third hole, and now I'm 12 over but I'm having a great time. After that I played pretty well and wound up shooting 95 and made some money. The caddie couldn't believe it.

Another time I played Prestwick, which is where the first twelve British Opens were played. I had 175 yards into a green with a four-foot drop in the middle. The caddie told me to make sure to hit it past the flag because the ball would roll back down toward the hole. I did just what he said but wound up four-putting. That's the thing about golf. Sometimes you get breaks you think you don't deserve, but when you get a bad break you have to think back to all the good breaks you got, too.

In what other ways do you think golf is like life?

Well, first of all, you're always making decisions and they won't all be good, but you also get a lot of second chances. About 80 percent of the time you have to take your punishment and move on, but about 20 percent of the time you can take a gamble and pull it off. If you can't accept making mistakes, don't play. You just have to keep trying. Like I always say, about 90 percent of life is just showing up.

Do people get nervous playing with you?

Sometimes in the beginning, which always amazes me, but eventually they relax.

Which presidents were the best golfers? I remember asking Jerry Ford how his game was after he left the presidency, and he said it was getting better because he was hitting fewer people.

I think FDR was probably the best. There's a photograph in his library of him hitting a shot, and you can tell he had a good swing. JFK was also very good, but he had back problems and he tried to conceal how good he was because it was still thought of as a rich man's sport.

Are there any courses you haven't played that you'd like to play?

Pine Valley and Augusta. I've also heard a lot of good things about the Sand Hills Golf Club in Nebraska. But really, the big thing is that I can have a good time on any golf course. I've reached the point in my life where I can relax and enjoy myself out there.

. . .

When you spend time with President Clinton, you can't help but be impressed by his sheer enthusiasm for life. He

genuinely likes people and has a great curiosity. Over the years he's obviously learned how to roll with the punches, and playing the game that he loves is one way he's able to do just that. Plus, on a personal note, I'd like to say he's one helluva golfer!

BEN CRENSHAW

I'VE ADMIRED BEN CRENSHAW for longer than I'd like to admit.

Ben is three years older than I. He joined the PGA Tour right out of the University of Texas in 1973, winning the first event he entered as a pro, the 1973 San Antonio Texas Open. Since I won the third event I entered on the LPGA Tour, I've always figured that we had something in common—except our putting strokes: his is long and flowing and mine is a constant work in progress.

Actually, our careers have shared a number of highs and lows. I think the biggest thing we have in common is that we approach the game with a certain spirituality. I know that when I won the 1980 U.S. Women's Open by nine strokes, I felt that I was being guided by a powerful force or spirit, although it was a survival test in one-hundred-plus weather. And I know Ben felt the same way after he won his second Masters Tournament, in 1995, just after the death of his longtime teacher, Harvey Penick.

Ben enjoyed a great amateur career. He was a member of the University of Texas team that won three straight NCAA Championships, and in 1972 he and his teammate and fellow Austin resident Tom Kite shared the individual title.

He and Tom went on to remarkably similar careers. Both won nineteen times on tour, and both captained Ryder Cup teams. Ben won two Masters Tournaments. Tom won the 1992 U.S. Open. Both are members of the World Golf Hall of Fame, and Ben serves as its spokesman. As important as their similar records is the fact that they both learned the game under the caring and watchful eye of the legendary Harvey Penick, the longtime professional at the Austin Country Club, who also taught LPGA greats Kathy Whitworth and Sandra Palmer.

I can't think of a player—pro or amateur—who can rival Ben's love for and knowledge of the game's history. That passion extends to golf course architecture; Ben has spent long hours studying the works and writings of the great architects. He and his partner, Bill Coore, are considered among the top course designers in the game today, and because I am involved in design work, I can really appreciate how brilliant they are.

Even as a junior golfer, Ben was a wonderful competitor. His long, graceful, flowing swing has always been a joy to watch, and, of course, he is one of the finest putters who ever lived. Still, as competitive as he was, Ben always stressed that tournament golf was only one aspect of the game that he loves so much. In that sense, just as in his life, which includes his wife, Julie, and their three daughters, Ben has achieved a remarkable balance that I admire.

I met Ben for dinner early in 2007 when he was in Valencia, California, for the AT&T Champions Classic. We began by comparing notes about our teachers. Like Ben, I had only one teacher, Walter Keller. Both he and Harvey Penick were teachers from the old school, and they inspired confidence and trust in us, which was something else Ben and I have in common.

.   .   .

My father was a good player, and he introduced my older brother and me to the game when I was seven and he was eight. But it was Harvey who really taught us how to play. Harvey always looked old to us, even when he was a young man. He just had a very authoritative look, but his delivery was very demure. He never once raised his voice, but he made you listen. He said only so much and no more. By that, I mean he told you what you needed to know at that time and no more.

Knowing that Mr. Penick had taught both Ben and Tom Kite at the same time, I was curious about how that had worked.

That was an example of Harvey's genius. He knew Tom was more detail-oriented and analytical than me and that Tom really loved to work on the driving range and practice tee, while I enjoyed playing. It takes an unbelievable teacher to sift out your individual information and needs. Harvey might tell Tom something that was perfectly correct but wouldn't have any bearing for me, and vice versa. It's just the same way Walter Keller might tell you something that would be good for you but might not be good for someone else, like a Sandra Palmer. The thing about teachers like Harvey and Walter Keller is that they encourage people to keep improving but they don't make it harder by turning it into a chore. They both recognized that we had a passion and love for golf and knew when not to push it. They understood that our motivation was going to come from inside of us.

It was clear that Harvey Penick's impact on Ben had gone far beyond developing his golf game, and I asked him about that.

Harvey lived a life of kindness and generosity. This man was a saint. I mean, he was the most lovable, humble individual you could imagine. He devoted his life to teaching and helping others improve their golf. His humility and kindness were astounding. My dad had a great expression about Harvey. He said, "Harvey is as tender as a dove's heart."

I asked Ben about his emotional victory in the 1995 Masters, which he won just days after serving as a pallbearer at Mr. Penick's funeral.

The only way I can describe it is that I had a lot of help from a lot of different places that week. I was just very much at peace.

I could definitely relate. Ben and I talked about how my mother, Lea, died just six months before I won the 1991 Nabisco Dinah Shore for an unprecedented third time and by a record nine strokes. Like Ben at Augusta, I played like I was guided by something much bigger than myself. Ben agreed that in these tournaments, we played with the most grace we'll ever have. It's as though we had the talent but someone else was pulling the strings.

It turned out that Mr. Penick was instrumental in helping Ben develop his admiration and respect for the life, career, and writings of Bobby Jones. Hero is an overused word these days, but it is fair to say that Jones—who many argue was the greatest golfer in history—is one of Ben's heroes. Herbert Warren Wind, the great writer, once observed: "In the opinion of many people, of all the great athletes, Jones came the closest to being what we call a 'great man.'" Ben once said that if there was just one person he'd love to have dinner with, it would be "Bob Jones, and not to talk about golf."

When I was growing up, Harvey told me he wanted me to "read whatever Bobby Jones has to say about the game," and I've read everything. Bobby Jones just made more sense to me than any golfer ever. He was just a brilliant writer. He was a very graceful person, and not just in the physical sense. He was a very rare human being in that he did things with so much substance and style and grace and good taste. His acceptance speeches are a perfect example of what I mean. They were very short and very modest.

Ben also pointed out that while Jones is the perfect example of a true sportsman, they both fought to overcome fierce tempers, particularly early in their careers.

Jones once wrote that golf is sometimes a game that is "impossible to endure with a club in your hands." He had a violent temper—I mean really violent. In the third round of the 1921 British Open at St. Andrews, he tore up his scorecard and walked off the course. But in the last three years of his career, you would never know he had a temper. Harvey once said to me, "Tempers aren't such a bad thing. You'll learn to temper it at some point." I'll admit I lost a lot of tournaments because of my temper. I couldn't get it out of my system.

Ben's respect for Jones extends to the course that Jones loved above all others, the Old Course at St. Andrews, which he lists among his favorites. I asked him why.

I just love the challenge it presents. It's like an outdoor game of Chinese checkers. It's such a fascinating test. I honestly believe you could play the Old Course every day for the rest of your life and still not learn everything about it.

When I asked Ben who would make up his ideal foursome, I wasn't surprised that he included Jones, but his two other choices were unexpected.

Old Tom Morris (the winner of the 1861, '62, '64, and '67 British Opens) would be one. He was obviously a wonderful player and he had a great generosity of spirit. After a round, if he had a couple of extra shillings he would give them to the caddies. He had a kindness for the caddies. *The Life of Tom Morris,* written by the Reverend W. W. Tulloch in 1908, is the most beautiful book you've ever seen. I'd also add Dr. Alister MacKenzie [the designer of some of the world's most respected courses, including the Augusta National Golf Club, which he codesigned with Bobby Jones] because it would be fascinating to walk around a course and listen to his insights and observations.

It's interesting to note that when I asked Ben where he'd like to play, he said Augusta National, Pine Valley, the Old Course, and Royal Melbourne—another MacKenzie design that incorporates the best of Scottish and American designs. This brought us to a discussion of his design philosophy.

You know, I've heard it said that almost everybody who plays the game would like to be involved in design in some way, so I guess I'm like everyone else. As for Bill Coore's and my thinking about design, I go back to something Donald Ross said: "Golf should be a pleasure, not a penance." I've always said that the easiest thing to do is to make a course more difficult. We don't like artificiality. Like Perry Maxwell said, "A golf course must be there, not brought there. You have to find it." But no matter what, one of the great things about golf is that it's going to inflict some real damage on you. And you know, no matter how good a player you are, the game's going to make you look like a fool at some point and sometimes in front of a lot of people.

As our dinner wound down, Ben became reflective.

Golf has always been an endless pursuit in learning, which is one reason I'm such a proponent of the game. It just teaches you so much. Its values are strong and it's been bridging the generation gaps for five or six hundred years. People ask why golf is like life, and I think it's because it's a long learning process that you never complete. I've had an idyllic life. Julie's such a wonderful mom, and my girls are all different. They've been so soothing. None of us has it all, but I've been luckier than most because of the people I've met. I think that when you boil it down, at the end of a person's life, what matters is family, friends, and relationships.

. . .

I love how Ben Crenshaw's passion for the game—a passion born of a unique gift, honed by a brilliant teacher, inspired by the zest for learning and life and the writings of a remarkable man, and pursued with unwavering determination—is interwoven with his passion for life. For both of us, spirituality has been an important part of our golf careers and lives.

KENNY G.

ONE OF MY NICKNAMES on the LPGA Tour is "Holly-wood" because I know so many people in the enter-tainment business. One of my favorites is Kenny G. (Kenneth Gorelick), one of the most successful musicians in the world. By mid-2006, he had sold forty-eight million albums, and I consider him a genius, whether he's playing the soprano saxophone, which is his primary instrument, or the alto sax, tenor sax, or flute. Kenny became intrigued with the saxo-phone when he saw a performer on the old *Ed Sullivan Show*. He learned to play by listening to records, particularly those of Grover Washington Jr.

But the Kenny G. I know is one of the best amateur golfers today. He and I are dear friends, and we've played a lot of golf around Southern California, usually with a little money on the line. The last time I looked, he had a plus-0.6 handicap, and in 2007, *Golf Digest* ranked him as the best golfing mu-sician in America. He's a fixture in the AT&T Pebble Beach

National Pro-Am, which he played in seven times through 2007, and that was what I asked him about at the beginning of our interview, which took place at his house in Malibu.

. . .

I know you came close to winning the team title at the 2001 AT&T. Tell me about it.

I was paired with Phil Mickelson, and we came to the last hole needing a par to beat Tiger Woods and his partner, Jerry Chang, who played on the golf team with him at Stanford. The problem was that Phil needed an eagle to beat Davis Love III and a birdie to tie for the individual title. He hit a good drive and decided to try to reach the green [on the par-5] in two. I had watched his short game for a week, and he was magical. He could have easily hit something down short of the green, pitched up, and made a birdie. But his mind-set back then was to always gamble and be aggressive. He tried to hit a driver off the deck, and he put it in the water. That meant everything was left up to me. We both had been choking our guts out, but I had to putt to win. I was really grinding over it and I hit a good putt. It literally went in the cup and spun out. The thing I learned from that was that I didn't embrace the moment. I didn't enjoy the pressure. But the next time I faced a similar situation was in the Michael Douglas Celebrity Tournament. I had another putt I needed to make, and

I told myself that I'd been in that position before and I could make the putt—and I did. The other good thing about the 2001 AT&T was that Jerry Chang and I became friends, and that gives me something to talk about with Tiger.

Is the AT&T your favorite event?

I love it. It's the Masters of pro-ams. I stay at Clint Eastwood's Mission Ranch, and you go down for breakfast in the morning and there are guys like Andy Garcia, Chris O'Donnell, and Peter Gallagher and you talk about your games and your partners. You go to the practice range and you get to ask these great players about their swings. Golf is just so amazing. How else could a guy like me meet Jack Nicklaus, Arnold Palmer, and Tiger Woods? I've played golf with President Clinton and the heads of major corporations. I even played golf in Monaco with Prince Albert. How great is that?

What's it like playing with Tiger?

It's the most fun. He is just supercool and cocky. He's brilliant and he loves a challenge. You know who one of the coolest guys I've ever played with is? Arnold Palmer. He's just awesome.

Did you play a match with him?

This is one of my all-time favorite stories. I was playing in the pro-am at his tournament at Bay Hill. First of all, he made me feel like I could totally be myself. And he's a real performer. He just loves the stage. We were playing at Isleworth and I beat him on the front nine. I was actually beating Arnie! It was just so casual and I was having a ball. He came up to me at the turn and asked me if I wanted to play for a dollar on the back. All of a sudden there was something on the line, and everything changed. He went 2-under on the back and I was about 10-over. I gave him the dollar and said, "You knew what you were doing, didn't you?" He said, "I've been playing golf for a long time and I don't like to lose." He totally got me. It was a great lesson.

Tell me how you got started in the game.

I was about ten. My brother was five years older than me and he took me to Jefferson Park Golf Course in Seattle, which is where Freddie Couples learned to play. The game appealed to me right from the beginning. It was like the saxophone. It was hard, but if you worked at it you were going to get it. That's the trick golf plays on you. You think you can master it, but you can't. You can come close to mastering an instrument, but not golf.

Golf is never the same from day to day.

Neither is the sax, although in that way it's a lot easier. Again, it's a trick. The sax looks harder than golf. People watch golf and they say, "Hey, I can do that," and that's how you get hooked.

Has golf always been serious for you, or have you ever engaged in any high jinks on the course?

I was the captain of my high school golf team. We were a pretty diverse school. You could always tell our team because we were the one that had black and Asian players. I remember playing in a tournament at a pretty exclusive club and I asked one of my best friends, Lee Turner, to caddie for me. He was a black kid and a tremendous drummer. I asked him to really dress like a pimp and he showed up in this amazing purple outfit. It was so distracting that I won my match. My opponent didn't have a chance.

Could you have been a pro?

If I had devoted the time and energy when I was younger, maybe. Now, at fifty, I don't think so. Again, good players look at the Champions Tour and think they could compete out there. It's a lot tougher than it looks. But I always wanted to play in a professional event, so I played in the Nationwide Tour. It wasn't pretty. The greens were so much faster than I was used to, and I couldn't figure them out. It gave me a lot of respect for Annika Sorenstam and Michelle Wie for trying to play on the PGA Tour. Again, it is so much harder than it looks.

Were your playing partners intimidated?

Not at all. I had sushi delivered to us on the sixth hole. They loved it. I shot two rounds in the 80s but had a lot of fun.

Do you remember the time we played the Augusta National? I remember that we were both so excited about playing that we were out on the putting green for an hour and a half the night before we played.

That's a perfect example of what I'm talking about. The greens were pretty slow. We played from the forward tees, and there was no rough. I was 1-under on the front nine. But having played the course, I can't even imagine how these guys play so well at the Masters. The greens are much faster and the course is so long. Take number eleven. We played it at about 375 yards. They play it at 480 yards. I'd have to lay up short of that green. They play a completely different game.

I know you like to have something on the line when you play golf. . . .

It doesn't have to be much, but I do like to play for enough to make myself a little nervous. I like the challenge of having a putt or a shot that means something. I recently played in the qualifying round for my club championship. I had a putt on the last hole. If I'd made it, I'd have beaten the three guys I was playing with, who were good players. It didn't have anything to do with qualifying. I really wanted to make that putt and was grinding over it. When I made it, it meant a lot to me.

A lot of people don't like that kind of pressure.

I like it because I think it's good for me. Most people don't care about getting better. They just want to enjoy themselves. That's fine, but I like putting myself in a position to improve. I like to stress myself out, not in a bad sense but in the sense that it helps me grow.

Like Fuzzy Zoeller said, "All I want is a chance to choke."

Yes, but only if you learn something from choking.

Do you feel the same pressure when you perform?

When I walk onstage, there's the pressure of knowing I only have one shot to play that song, and I like that pressure. But it's different because I know I have it. I might not always play every note perfectly, but I go into the concert thinking I will. Plus, I like the challenge and excitement of putting myself on the line. That's how you get better. You always have to test yourself.

It's like a golfer facing a flop shot over a bunker with a lot of money on the line. There's a part of you that knows, deep down, whether you've prepared yourself. Like John Wooden [the legendary UCLA basketball coach] said, the key to success is preparation. You have to work harder than everyone else. It's part of the karma to greatness.

Exactly. That's why I love the learning process in golf and with my music. I don't want playing good to be random. With the sax, I have the mechanics down. Do I play great all the time? No. Do I play bad all the time? No. But do I play really good most of the time? Absolutely. You're that way in golf. For me, when it comes to golf, I play great sometimes, but most of the time I play what I consider mediocre golf. My mechanics aren't there yet.

Are you a perfectionist?

My fun is mastering the learning process. That's something I love. If I'm doing something at the same level and not improving, it's not that much fun. When you and I play, I'm always learning something just from observing. To me, golf is just like learning an instrument. I honestly believe that if you work hard enough, you can get really good at it.

Do you ever think you suffer from paralysis by analysis?

I'll tell you a great story. I'm pretty self-taught, but I've become friends with Butch Harmon. I played at his wedding and he offered to help me anytime I asked. He stayed at my beach house one time and we drank some really good Bordeaux and he said to me, "You know that golf studio you have in your house? Get rid of it. It's making you worse." My teacher had been telling me that for years, so I finally got rid of it. And do you know what? They were right. I just think I'm pretty intense in everything I do. I could use a little more couch-potato time.

When you practice the sax, is it similar to the way you practice golf?

When I'm at home, I take the kids to school and I come home and practice the sax for about two hours. I practice until I feel like my mouth is going to fall off. People don't realize that a performer has to stay in condition. At about ten-thirty I head to the course. I might work on four or five things. I used to be a real range rat, but now I like to actually play more. Again, I just love the learning process. I love trying to figure out how each part of the swing affects the other parts.

Do you think there are comparisons between your golf and your music?

Well, you have to master the mechanics, but I think when I'm performing, I don't have a lot of specific thoughts, like I have swing thoughts in golf. I'm just playing the music. That's where I'm trying to get to in golf. I just want to play.

I love creating shots. It's like an art. The big thing is just to enjoy myself when I'm playing golf like I enjoy myself when I'm performing. When I'm totally relaxed, I play golf pretty well. When I think about it, I get nervous.

Has golf made your life better?

It's made me a better person. Now I realize that life isn't perfect and I can't control it. I used to try to have complete control of my life, and I'd get upset if things didn't go as I planned. I began to realize through golf that sometimes you can't get it all together. Sometimes you hit a perfect drive and it lands in a gopher hole. Now, when things don't go just right, I say, well, it's just one of those days, and play on.

.   .   .

I've always sensed that there is a similarity between playing really good golf and being a talented musician. At the highest levels, golfers and musicians are both artists and performers. I've told Kenny that I think he's good enough to win the California State Amateur, which is a championship that draws a lot of top players. But to do that, he'd have to let himself go and play golf the way he plays music. He has to let the dancer become the dance. It's one thing to be a perfectionist in golf and life, but sometimes you just have to let go and trust your instincts.

DENNIS HOPPER

I T'S SAID THAT "golf is the game of a lifetime," but in
Dennis Hopper's case, it might be the game that saved
his life.

I met Dennis at the complex he calls home in Venice,
California. The place, which he shares with his fifth wife,
Victoria Duffy, and their children, resembles a huge metal
fortress. The exterior does not lend a hint to what lies beyond the metal walls. The complex is actually a couple of
loft studios and a metal silo that houses Hopper's enormous
art collection, which includes works by Julian Schnabel,
Jean-Michel Basquiat, Richard Serra, Andy Warhol, and
many others. One of the lofts was originally designed by
architect Frank Gehry and then adapted as a living space
by architect Brian Murphy. Murphy and Hopper also collaborated on a building that Hopper refers to as the "Art
Barn." He has since bought another Gehry studio, and
Murphy linked the two, knocking out walls and building

a connecting staircase. A few years ago, Dennis bought a neighboring California Craftsman house that serves as a guest cottage with a pool and Jacuzzi. There are toys everywhere, in interesting juxtaposition to the $8-million-plus art collection that adorns the space. He is clearly settled in his role as husband and father.

Dennis met me downstairs, and we went up to the loft area. As we ascended the stairs, I noticed a few motorcycles along with several cars in an open garage area. I asked him if he still rode. "Not very often," he said.

Upstairs was spacious and equally eclectic, with very few windows. Dennis's wife was seated at her desk, working on the computer. Before I arrived, Dennis had been sitting on his second-floor terrace enjoying a cigar and sipping tea from a cup with a golf motif.

At age seventy, he remains strikingly handsome—trim and youthful, with gray hair and blue eyes, casually dressed in a shirt and slacks. He absolutely does not look like a man who struggled with drugs and alcohol through his adult years.

I quickly discovered that Dennis Hopper, the prolific filmmaker, actor, director, painter, and photographer, is as complex and interesting as the art collection he has assembled.

I began by asking him how he came to golf relatively late in life and about the role it played in his recovery from alcoholism.

. . .

My father tried to get me interested in the game when I was a kid. He was a hardworking guy, and he didn't have a lot of time to be with me. The couple of times I tried to play with him, I hated it. I thought it was a game for sissies and I didn't want any part of it. I was an idiot. I still am an idiot, but I'm an older idiot now.

Anyway, when I was about forty-eight, I was just getting over my alcoholism—if you ever get over it. I had just started in Alcoholics Anonymous and I was down in Austin, Texas. Willie Nelson invited me to come down to his place in Perdenales, where he has his own nine-hole course. He said, "Golf will keep you out of the bars. We don't give lessons down there, Dennis. You just keep hitting the ball until you hear the turkey gobble [hole a putt]." I took him up on it and started hitting the ball around and pretty soon I could hit the ball pretty straight and sometimes I got to hear the turkey gobble. Willie invited [former University of Texas football coach] Darryl Royal and his wife, Edith, over to kind of babysit me. They're just wonderful people. He'd take me around the course but he never tried to give me lessons. I had the worst habits in the world, but I just stuck with it. It kept me going and I really got into it. I just loved the game, and it's been a good friend to me. I can't describe it as anything else. It's very frustrating not to play very well, but it's also something that gets me outside, gets me with friends, gets me competitive, and it gives me something to think about. Golf really makes me feel good and gives me a great joy in my life.

I felt a little awkward but asked him if he found golf addictive.

Oh, it is addictive. I replaced one addiction—or maybe a few addictions—with it, so I know it is addictive. I mean, I woke up this morning and the first thing I did was put on The Golf Channel. Besides, I'm seventy years old. What else am I going to get addicted to?

Do any of your children play?

I've tried to get my son, who's fifteen, interested in the game, but it's not taking. I've had him riding around in carts since he was two. I'd like him to play because I think the game builds character. I look at all the young people taking up the game and it teaches them to be civilized. I mean, you're out there with clubs in your hands and you're not hitting each other. It teaches you courtesy, honesty, and how to behave. I see kids out there who are just running but they become very disciplined on the golf course. They learn to be quiet when others are hitting, and the etiquette you learn from golf is so related to the way people should deal with each other in life.

The other great thing about golf is that it teaches you that life is not easy because golf isn't easy. You can go as far as you want in both life and golf, but you've got to really work at it. Golf is one of the most difficult games in the world—if not the most difficult. The more I get to know about it, the more I realize how little I really know about it. Every time I think I've really got it, I realize I've lost it by the next hole, so in that way it teaches you patience. And it can teach you optimism. If you have a bad hole, there's always another one coming up.

In terms of teaching honesty, I don't understand people who cheat. When I see someone cheating I think it's just kind of sad. I think they're really just cheating themselves.

Both Dennis and I are members of Riviera Country Club in Pacific Palisades. It's kind of been my home course since I was a junior golfer and used to sneak under the fence to practice. When I was fifteen, the club was kind enough to give me playing privileges so I could play with the members' kids. I was curious about when he had joined.

I wanted to join Riviera, and when I first tried to get in, I think it cost about $26,000 or $28,000. Then the club was sold and the membership was closed down. Then it was sold again, and I got in about 1993. It took me about ten years, and the price went up to about $78,000. In the meantime,

I tried to join Sherwood Country Club, just north of L.A. They wanted $250,000. I don't know what I was thinking. I'm glad they turned me down.

We talked about his early days in Hollywood.

The first movie I made was *I Died a Thousand Deaths,* with Jack Palance and Shelley Winters. Then I did *Rebel Without a Cause,* with James Dean. I was eighteen. The next year we made *Giant.* I don't think Dean played golf but he was a good athlete. His team won the state basketball championship when he was in high school. He was basically interested in racing cars. Back then, about the only person I knew who played golf was Jim Garner, and he could really play.

Is there a connection between golf and acting?

I remember one year when I was under contract with Warner Bros. and Jack Warner brought in all these great young athletes he wanted to put under contract. He had some of us meet with them. I asked them what was the most important thing about playing a sport. They all said staying relaxed. I said it's the same in acting. You've got to stay relaxed. You've got to know where your tension areas are so you can react in a moment-to-moment reality level with the people you're acting with. I've just discovered that when I relax and just swing, I can hit the ball thirty yards farther and much straighter. Now my last swing thought is to just stay relaxed.

There is another similarity that I've thought of recently: when I watch Tiger Woods, it's like watching a great film-maker that's on a roll. It's exactly the same thing. You just know there are going to be some exceptional moments. It's just a privilege to watch them.

Would you be totally intimidated by playing with Tiger?

No, I think it would probably be okay. It wouldn't bother me because my game has absolutely nothing to do with his, that's for sure.

. . .

When I look back on my conversation with Dennis Hopper, I think about the importance of pursuing your passions. In his case, it is love of the arts and of golf. He is clearly attracted to the beauty and artistry of both. He is probably more talented as an artist and actor, but that doesn't mean he loves golf any less. I was also struck by the fact that while he took up the game late in life, he pursues it with the fascination and enthusiasm I remember feeling as a kid, when I was learning the game by knocking balls around the front yard and putting into soup cans. Actually, I'm not surprised that someone who loves art the way Dennis does would be attracted to golf. I've always viewed

hitting golf shots—fades, draws, high and low shots, little shots around the greens—as an art form. Practicing for me was like a painter working to get the shades and tones just right. Like art, golf requires a freedom of expression and a mastery of style.

STEVE KROFT

U NLIKE MANY of the other people I interviewed for
this book, Steve Kroft, the Emmy Award–winning
correspondent for *60 Minutes,* is someone I met fairly
recently.

We met in the spring of 2007 at his office on the far
West Side of Manhattan, and it looked just like I'd always imagined a journalist's office should look. The wall
behind his very cluttered desk was lined with books and
with mementos of his life and career, including a Cleveland
Browns helmet (a symbol of his deep midwestern roots).
On the opposite wall, above the couch where I sat during
the interview, were pictures that reflected his accomplishments and interests, including a photo of Steve with Walter Cronkite on the eighteenth green at the National Golf
Links on the far end of New York's Long Island, where he
has been a member since 1998. From his desk, writing at
his computer, he has a beautiful view of the Hudson River.

His Emmy statuettes sat modestly atop a radiator. I liked that. It was a nice touch that told me something about the man, that he didn't take himself too seriously.

He does take his work seriously, though.

After graduating from Syracuse University in 1967 with a degree in mass communications, he was drafted into the army and did a tour in Vietnam, worked briefly at a television station in Syracuse, then received his master's from the prestigious Columbia University Graduate School of Journalism. After jobs at local stations in Florida, he joined CBS News in 1980, working in New York City, Dallas, and Miami, before joining the London bureau. In 1986 he returned to New York to become a principal correspondent for a new magazine program, *West 57th Street*. When that program was canceled in 1989, he joined *60 Minutes.*

In all, he has won nine Emmy Awards, including the 2002 Lifetime Achievement Award he received as part of the *60 Minutes* team. He has also won three Peabody Awards.

Since he is more used to asking questions than answering them, I was happy to discover that he was not only easy to spend time with but very happy to talk about the role golf has played in his life. I began by asking him how he'd been introduced to the game.

. . .

I grew up in Kokomo, Indiana. My father, Fred, was a very good amateur golfer. He played at Purdue, won the club championship at Kokomo Country Club about ten times, and was very influential in the Indiana Golf Association. He was friends with some great amateurs like Ed Tutwiler and Dale Morey, as well as Pete and Alice Dye before they really became involved in golf course architecture. He always said his priorities were his family, his job, and golf, but I'm not really sure that was always the order. Anyway, from an early age I was surrounded by golf and golfers.

I didn't really take up the game until I was twelve. By that time I was too old for Little League and too small for football, so I moved on to golf. I would ride my bike to the club and play all day long. I loved it. My father was a lifer at Union Carbide. He started working in the local plant when he was very young and eventually became a corporate vice president for mining and metals. That meant playing a lot of customer golf, and he had memberships at Pine Valley, San Francisco Golf Club, and Laurel Valley. When I was sixteen, he was transferred east and we moved to Chappaqua, New York, where we joined Whippoorwill Country Club, which has a wonderful old Donald Ross course.

Like a lot of kids, I learned the game from my father. He had learned from his father, so that makes sense. I wanted to be like my father. A friend of mine once said that playing in father-son tournaments probably paid more psychiatrists' bills than anything else, and that might be true. When I played with him I just felt so much pressure not to let him down.

I played at Syracuse, which is not exactly a hotbed of college golf. I was probably a 4- or 5-handicapper, and most of the guys on the team were in that range. The great thing about Syracuse was that you learned to play in the snow and sleet. Basically, if you didn't freeze solid, you were fine.

After college, I served in Vietnam, and for about the next ten years I played very little, maybe four or five times a year, and most of the time I played it was when I was visiting my parents and would play with my dad. I came to CBS in 1980 and to *60 Minutes* in 1989. Golf was viewed—if not with contempt—at least as an eccentric pastime at CBS, particularly at *60 Minutes.* [Former executive producer] Don Hewitt, Mike Wallace, and Morley Safer all played tennis and didn't have much use for golf.

I really started playing more golf once I came to *60 Minutes* because we have the entire month of July off. My wife, Jennet, and I have a house in Sag Harbor, and there are so many great courses in the Hamptons (Shinnecock Hills, National Golf Links, Maidstone, the Atlantic Golf Club, and Sebonack) that it gave me a lot of places to play. I joined the National in 1998 because I knew more members there and loved the course. Because of the wind, it plays differently every day. I probably play fifty to sixty rounds a year and fluctuate between a 7- and an 8-handicap. I have three or four regular games, but I like to mix it up and play with as many different people as possible. It's interesting to observe people on the golf course. It's a great revealer of character. You see how they react to pressure and adversity. You also see how well they count and what they do in the rough or the woods if they think no one is watching.

I'm a grinder on the golf course, and I suppose that's the way I approach the pieces I do for *60 Minutes.* You just have to do the best you can with what you have, and on the golf course, that means accepting the bad shot or the bad break and moving on to the next shot. That's not always easy to do, but when you watch the great players, that's a trait they seem to have in common.

I noticed Steve's photo of himself with Greg Norman on a golf course. I asked him if he had done many features on golfers.

Not really. That photo was taken at the Carnegie Club at Skibo Castle in Scotland when we were doing a piece on Greg Norman that ran in 1997, a year after he lost the Masters to Nick Faldo in such a dramatic fashion. The focus of the piece was his business success, but I wanted to get him to discuss his loss to Faldo. He was very reluctant to talk about it, and initially refused altogether. Eventually he did, but he seemed determined to put it out of his mind and move on with his life. I thought that was very revealing. I also did a piece on Michelle Wie. People wonder if her parents or agents are pushing her and if she's trying to do too much, too fast. I never got the sense that she was being pushed. Were the expectations too high? Probably. But then it's hard to say no to all the celebrity and wealth. It will be interesting to see how it all turns out.

Another quasi–golf piece I did was on Clint Eastwood, whom we've profiled twice. He's a fantastic guy. He's very complicated and yet down to earth, which I really wasn't expecting. He's so talented on so many different levels—as an actor, a director, and in business. And he's passionate about golf. We played Cypress Point and it was one of the best days I've ever had on a golf course.

Another photo on his bookcase is of his son. I asked if he was a golfer, too.

John is thirteen and I think this summer might be when he begins to really take an interest in golf. He picked up tennis from his mother. Like my mother, she doesn't play golf but she's really supportive of my playing. It's interesting seeing the game through John's eyes. I want to teach him things like controlling his temper and playing one shot at a time, staying in the present—all things I know but need to work on myself. They're things I want to pass on to him—along with the love of the game I learned from my father.

. . .

Thinking back on my time with Steve, I was struck by how great an influence golf has been in his family—a sport and a love passed down from his grandfather to his father, to him, and now to his son. It reminded me very much of a quotation from the Talmud, the Jewish book of prayer. I came across it many years ago, and it has always had a deep meaning for me: "Whoever teaches his son teaches not alone his son but also his son's son, and so on to the end of generations."

LESLIE MOONVES

L ESLIE MOONVES is president and chief executive officer of CBS Corporation, but when first meeting him, you might not guess that he leads one of the world's largest and most well-known media companies. He's energetic and focused but also friendly and relaxed—not the typical image many people have of your average Fortune 500 CEO.

I first met Les several years ago at Riviera in Los Angeles, and I was immediately struck by what a jovial person he is. Now we more often see each other at Bel-Air, where we are both members. Unfortunately, though, he doesn't get to play there as much as he'd like, since he divides his time between New York City and L.A. and has such a busy schedule.

When I think of Les, the memory that stands out most is of our time together at the "Lemons and Swells" party, an annual putting tournament party hosted by mutual friends who live in Malibu. The Swells (which include Les and his wife, Julie, as well as other prominent Hollywood types) and the Lemons (their less high-flying friends) attend this casual competition held on our friends' backyard putting green. A couple of years ago I played in a pair behind Les and got a close look at his putting stroke. Watching him putt and talking to him afterward, I could tell that he has a true reverence for the game and understands it as both a competitor and an artist. A great sense of humor, confidence, and the abilities to focus, manage your emotions, and be competitive are all traits necessary for success as a golfer and a business leader, and they are all a part of Les.

It was therefore less surprising to learn that his first career goal was to be an actor. While he went on to perform in many stage and television productions, he quickly realized there wasn't a lot of job security in that line of work and decided to pursue his passion for the business in another way. Now as head of CBS, he oversees all of its divisions, including its broadcast and cable television, radio, digital media, publishing, film, and outdoor advertising businesses. Highlights from his career as a television executive include greenlighting some of the most successful programs ever, such as CBS's *Survivor, CSI: Crime Scene Investigation,* and *Everybody Loves Raymond,* and before that *ER* and *Friends.* He's received many honors and awards over the years, but to me, having been named

Entertainment Weekly's "Most Powerful Man in Hollywood" best sums up his achievements.

That said, it was the unassuming Les I knew from Bel-Air and the putting tournament party I had in mind when I joined him for our interview at his office at the CBS headquarters in New York. The suite, on the thirty-fifth floor, was originally the office of William S. Paley, the founder of CBS.

I began by asking him how he got started in golf.

. . .

I didn't start playing until I was in my late thirties or early forties. I played a lot of baseball as a kid, and then as I got older I focused on tennis and softball. I was really competitive in both, and really played very little golf as a kid. It's a funny thing—I'm a natural right-hander but I always batted left-handed. When I took up golf, it just felt more natural to play as a lefty. I think playing baseball and softball carried over to golf. Dave Podas, the professional at Bel-Air, gave me a great piece of advice. I was always told that a baseball swing and a golf swing had nothing in common. Podas disagreed with that completely. They are more alike than people think, especially when a golf swing involves rolling my forearms over. That was a great help.

Why did you wait until a relatively late age to take up golf?

Between my career and my family, it was hard to find the time. To this day, I have never played a good round on a weekday, probably because I feel I should be working. On weekends it's different. I find golf therapeutic. It gets my mind off work.

Do you like the social aspect of the game?

When in L.A., I have a regular weekly game, which I enjoy. Good friends, good camaraderie. It's hard to find time for that in New York. I love Bel-Air. It's very peaceful because each hole is secluded. You don't see a lot of people.

Are there any courses you haven't played that you'd really like to try?

I'm very lucky—I've been able to play so many courses because CBS is so involved with golf. I love Pebble Beach because the views are so magnificent. Augusta National is the course I enjoy the most. The first time I saw the place, it stunned me. It was like something out of *The Wizard of Oz*. It is just so beautiful. It's like the White House. I get a special feeling every time I'm there. I've played the great courses in Scotland. The one course I'd really like to play is Cypress Point. I just think you can get a sense of the spirit of a city or a place when you play a golf course there. And I like that every golf course is different. In tennis, pretty much every court is the same.

You're obviously in a very competitive business. Does that carry over to the golf course?

My life is very competitive. I get the overnight ratings every morning at six. I work twenty-four/seven. When stock analysts say to me, "Have you thought of this . . ." I stop them right away and tell them there's nothing I haven't thought of. I'm competitive on the golf course but I never get angry. It's interesting, but when I stand over a shot it's very peaceful. If something troublesome comes into your head, you can get it out. At the end of the day, whether I've played well or not, I'm refreshed.

What's the state of your game?

I'm a 17 but I'm a good money player. Guys like to have me as their partner because I'm good for four or five pars a round and I make good shots under pressure. I'll give you an example: I was playing with Bill Clinton at Riviera. We're on the first tee and there's a big crowd behind the tee. I just thought, "Please, just let me hit a good shot." Sure enough, I hit a great drive. Of course, I hit my second shot into a barranca.

What do you like best about your job?

I get to meet such interesting people. I'm very proud to be part of the world of golf. I like being in the production trucks during a golf telecast. I've gotten a few lessons from Peter Kostis, which is great. I'd love to play a round with [CBS golf analyst] Nick Faldo.

I imagine that can be arranged. . . .

. . .

Like other powerful, successful people, Les Moonves respects golf as something that can never be mastered but can be enjoyed as a way to relax, pause, and refresh yourself, either alone on the course or with friends. The pressure he's under at CBS is enormous, and through golf he's able to decompress. I know that when I was playing in tournaments, I found cooking very relaxing. It was my way of easing the pressures of competition. In fact, as a lark I used to work as a short-order cook at a restaurant in Los Angeles called the Butterfly Bakery. It could get pretty hectic at times, but it never bothered me. The pressure of getting a sandwich made just right for a customer on a half-hour lunch break was tougher than facing a downhill three-footer to win, but I loved every second of it—and still do, if anyone is looking for a good sous chef. . . .

JIM NANTZ

B Y ANY STANDARD, Jim Nantz is the most accomplished and most versatile announcer working in television today. Since joining CBS Sports in 1985, he has served as anchor and/or lead play-by-play announcer for the Super Bowl, the Winter Olympics, major college-football games, and the NCAA basketball's Final Four. In 1995 he became anchor for the network's golf coverage, including the Masters Tournament, an important event that transcends sports and that is dear to his heart. Jim is a two-time winner of the National Sportscaster of the Year Award, and in 2002 he became the youngest winner of the Naismith Memorial Basketball Hall of Fame's Curt Gowdy Media Award.

Jim and I have known each other for years, dating back to when he covered the LPGA for CBS. We met for breakfast at Bel-Air Country Club in Los Angeles when he was in town for the telecast of the 2007 Nissan Open. Jim has been coming to L.A. to cover the tournament since he joined the CBS golf family in 1986, and we often see each other when he's on the West Coast. He fell in love with Bel-Air, and he likes nothing better than to sit at the "smart table" in the grill room and visit with the members. It's sarcastically called the smart table because the expression goes that the longer you sit there, the smarter you become. We have another expression at the smart table: "Pull up a chair if you don't have something nice to say about someone."

I asked Jim when he first realized that he wanted to be a broadcaster. Initially, his answer surprised me, but as we spoke, and I realized how much he truly loves his job, it made perfect sense.

. . .

From the time I was a kid, I was smitten by voices. I loved to listen to people like Jim McKay, Jack Whitaker, Pat Summerall, and so many others, not because they were announcers but because they were storytellers. I knew that's what I wanted to do. I wanted to tell stories about people and places and other cultures. And the only place I ever wanted to work was CBS because they had the best storytellers. And they had the Masters. It was always my dream to broadcast the Masters.

And that dream came true in 1986 . . .

And what a year to have it come true. That was the year Jack [Nicklaus] won his last Masters by shooting a 30 on the back nine on Sunday. Everything about it was magical. His son, Jackie, was on the bag. People had written him off, and the Bear had come out of hibernation. There's a particular memory I'll always treasure. I was walking back to the CBS compound, and Ken Venturi stopped and picked me up in his cart. He told me, "Kid, you may go on to broadcast fifty more Masters, but you'll never see another one as great as this."

I wondered if Jack's win in 1985 was even more special than Jim's college roommate Fred Couples's win in 1992.

Fred's win was obviously much more personal. When we were in college, we used to pretend that I was interviewing him in Butler Cabin after he won the Masters. It was never after he won the Open or PGA. It was always the Masters. It was pretty tough holding it together during the Green Jacket ceremony, and once we were off the air, we just hugged each other and cried.

We spoke about his collegiate golf career, and I was surprised by the intensity of his feelings. On the air, Jim is cool, calm, and collected. But when we spoke about his days at the University of Houston, I saw how much his experience there affected him.

I'd like to set the record straight because so much has been written about me being on the Houston golf team. I roomed with Fred, Blaine McCallister, and John Horne, who was actually the most decorated freshman that year. I didn't have a scholarship. I was a pretty good player. No false modesty. I really was pretty good. But I wasn't in their league and I never kidded myself that I was. If I had any thoughts that I was, they were stripped away pretty quickly. In August, Dave Williams, our coach, took us out to Sugarland Country Club. It was the first time we freshmen played in front of each other. The first hole was a reachable par-5. I wanted to try to get under par early, and I wound up making a double. I shot an 81. The other guys shot in the low 70s. They just didn't miss many shots, and when they did, their misses weren't bad misses. I had never really thought about playing professionally, but that day pretty much convinced me that I wasn't going to play college golf, at least not for Houston. The truth is, even though it was brief, the time I played at Houston has haunted me for years. People expected—or at least I thought they expected—me to go out and shoot 72 every time. I knew I couldn't do that, given my work schedule. I didn't want to put my game on display and shoot in the 80s or maybe higher. As a result, for a long time I limited myself to playing only with friends.

The one really great thing that came out of my time at Houston was the relationship I developed with Dave

Williams. He was a fantastic coach. His teams won six-teen NCAA Championships in thirty years. But he was much more than a coach. I would place him up there with [UCLA basketball coach] John Wooden and [Indianapolis Colts coach] Tony Dungy. They are all quiet, soft-spoken men, but when you're around them there's something spiritual, even saintly, about them.

Jim's life has been graced by strong relationships with older men—not the least of whom is his father.

Making my parents proud was always a driving force for me. When you look at how much love your parents give you, it can't help but make you whole as a person. I know that it helps me put people in a positive light, to see the good in them. I'm very close to both my parents. My mother is still active but my father hadn't been well for a while, and he died in 2008. My dad was in the tower with me at Colonial in 1995 and he had a stroke. He was sixty-six at the time. The irony was that we were looking forward to traveling together to the different events I was doing, and there he was at Colonial when it happened. One minute everything was perfect, and then . . .

It's hard for me to realize that one-seventh of his years were lost to the stroke. Sometimes when I visited him, he'd look at me as though he recognized me and smile, and then in a split second he was gone. When I was on the air, the TV was always on in his room. Did he hear me? I don't know. But I do know this: people ask me, "When you're doing the Super Bowl do you ever think that there are 140 million people tuned in?" I never thought about it. I was talking to only one person: my father.

In 2006, when Earl Woods was dying, I could completely relate to what Tiger was going through. Like my father and me, they couldn't have been closer. The relationship between a father and son is special. It's hard to explain. So is the relationship between a father and daughter [Jim and his wife, Lorrie, have a daughter, Caroline], but because of my relationship with my father, whenever I get tickets to major events like the Final Four, I always give a pair to a father and his son.

A man who figures prominently in Jim's life is Ken Venturi, the 1964 U.S. Open champion, who was his longtime broadcast partner in the eighteenth tower.

I've been lucky in terms of the people I broadcast with. Billy Packer and I have been together for twenty-two years. Phil Simms and I have been doing the NFL since 2002, and, of course, Kenny and I were together for seventeen years. There's a comfortable fit with all of them, and a trust factor.

Ken's been gone from CBS for five years, and people really miss us on-air together. He hears it from people all the time, and so do I. Part of the reason for our success was a generational thing, but people also sensed a deep friendship. We both have a great reverence for the game, and sometimes we'd just get lost in the moment. When we were on-air, it was as though it was two good friends who really loved the game just sitting there having a conversation. It was very special.

Another person Jim is very close to is former president George H. W. Bush.

Since my dad's stroke he's been more than a good friend. He's been like a surrogate father to me. We've probably played a hundred rounds of golf together. We talk all the time. He's obviously brilliant, and there's something very powerful about him, but there's something very soft and genteel about him as well. One of the great experiences of my life came in 2005. The president called me and said he wanted to invite former president Clinton to his house in Maine for a couple of days. They were going to play some golf and horseshoes and go out on the boat. Now, when two former presidents get together socially, it's interesting, to say the least. I think President Bush wanted me there as a third party, someone they'd both be comfortable with. We had a fabulous time. It couldn't have been better. In fact, the next year President Clinton came back for another visit and President Bush asked me to join them again. He asked me if I could find a fourth for golf, so I suggested [Patriots quarterback] Tom Brady. Forty-one was genuinely excited. One of his greatest qualities is his enthusiasm. He asked me if I thought I could really get Tom to join us. I told him it would be hard to say no to two former presidents. It was a dream foursome and we had a great time.

I asked Jim what was most special about golf for him.

As a kid, I played most of my golf with retirees, and, looking back, it taught me so much about respect and etiquette and how you should conduct yourself; about how to communicate and find a common ground with others. I think that's a wonderful lesson for a young person.

I think golf gives people a great appreciation for life itself. Golfers tend to see the small details and nuances. There's just something about being on a golf course—you don't even have to be playing—that grounds you. I don't know, it gives you a certain perspective. Every year, when I finish Sunday's broadcast from the AT&T, I go for a walk by myself at Cypress Point. To the right of the seventeenth green there's a plaque that was dedicated to Francis Beardsen in 1998. It reads: "Let us pause and give thanks for being one of the few to walk these magnificent shores." I love that.

Finally, golf teaches you to be humble. Humility is a wonderful trait. Arrogance doesn't wear well. If you're lucky, golf will make humility part of your nature.

.   .   .

Jim Nantz eloquently described the importance of humility. When you are successful in any walk of life, it's very easy to lose perspective. There are always people around to tell you how wonderful you are. Some of them actually believe it. You can enjoy wealth and privileges you might never have thought possible. One of my favorite stories about humility was told by the late—and truly, truly great—Harvey Penick. One day he came back from a seminar and said to his wife, Helen: "Just imagine, fifty of the game's greatest teachers all in one room."

"Harvey," his wife said, "there was one less great teacher there than you think."

Beautiful.

JACK NICHOLSON

ONCE HE FIGURED OUT that he couldn't be a professional athlete and before he decided to go into acting, Jack Nicholson wanted to be a sportswriter. While he
was at Manasquan (New Jersey) High School, he wrote basically the entire sports section of the school newspaper.
Being a sportswriter was an extension of his love of sports.
By his own admission, he was a "viciously competitive"
player and that carried over to his acting career.

I learned all this when we sat down for an interview
in his house on Mulholland Drive in Los Angeles, where
his love for art is on display. Nicholson is among the most
honored actors working today. His three Academy Awards
(he's been nominated for twelve) place him one behind
Katharine Hepburn, the winner of the most Oscars. He
famously guards his privacy but agreed to be interviewed
because we have played golf together many times and become friends. I think he just wanted to talk about golf with

a kindred spirit, and since he is such a raconteur, he wanted to know how my book was going to be different from the thousands of others about the game. Our conversation was fascinating, and not just the part about golf. Still, aware of his passion and respect for the game, I was surprised to discover that he had taken it up relatively late in life.

. . .

When I was growing up in New Jersey, if you didn't belong to a country club, you didn't play golf. I knew about Hogan and Snead and those guys, but my real love was team sports, especially basketball. That's a great sport because you can play one-on-one or with any number of players. That's why when you drive around L.A., you see people playing all over the place. Baseball is a great game, but you've got to find enough guys to have two teams.

Once I became a little successful, I decided to take up the rich boy's sports. I learned tennis when I was in my twenties and skiing in my thirties, which is about the same time I took up women in a big way and earned my reputation. But what the hell, I'm a no-regrets kind of guy. I did what I wanted to do, and still do. Like my friend Elmer Valentine said, there are two kinds of people in the world: those who score and don't know it, and those who score and know it. I know it.

I took up golf in my early fifties. I was making *The Two Jakes*, and I needed to look like a golfer. So I took some lessons at Whitsett Golf Course in Studio City, and right from the beginning the pro told me, "Jack, this game is going to bite you." He was right. Golf is like a drug. I played like a maniac. I've seen that happen to a lot of guys. They give up their marriages and their careers.

The thing is, guys who quit the game can be just as fanatical. I've had friends who were good players who just gave it up. I'd ask them to play, and they wouldn't. I couldn't figure it out. Then I realized that they had lost the ability to play as well as they used to and couldn't get it back. I don't know if it was a mental thing or what, but I guess they just didn't want to torture themselves.

Since Jack was a good athlete, I asked him if the game had been easy for him to pick up, especially at a late stage in life.

I don't think it's an easy game for anyone to pick up at any age, but it's probably more difficult as you get older. I was lucky because from the time I was a kid I've had an abnormal ability to concentrate. So when I'm on the course, I can focus completely on golf. I can't think about anything else. That's why golf has been so important to me when I've had an emotional crisis to deal with. For the four hours I'm on the course, golf is my focus. When I'm playing, I don't pay any attention to anyone else and I never listen to advice. I don't want people giving me advice. I don't even want to hear someone else getting advice. And I never gamble.

I want to enjoy the game in its purest state. As an actor, I always want to improve, and it's the same as a golfer. I'm out there to improve, and everything else is a distraction. That's one reason I never play in celebrity pro-ams and those kinds of things. I don't like playing with professionals very much. Why spend the day watching some guy hit it 150 yards past me? I don't want to waste the round.

I asked him about his best round.

About six or eight years ago I got to the point where I was consistently playing right around par. That's when I was playing like a maniac, three or four times a week. The best round I ever shot was a 65 at Lakeside. There are some great courses out here, but Lakeside is the toughest par in L.A. from the back tees. It has small greens with lots of variety. The last three holes on each nine are killers. You have to be very precise. That day I had a game plan and I stuck to it. I was 3-under after seven. It wasn't in a tournament, so there wasn't that much pressure, but after that round I couldn't break 80 for years. Now I'm an 85 shooter. I realized that I couldn't work as hard on my game as I needed to if I was going to take it up the next few notches.

I asked if he had continued to take a lot of lessons.

There are nine million books on golf. I listen to everything on television. I learn a lot from watching. I played in a tournament once with three other guys. One guy had a tremendous swing. It was very long. A thing of beauty. The other two had short swings, but they could both drive it about 285 yards. There were a lot fewer things that could go wrong with their swings, so I said to myself, "Parallel? Forget it." Golf's simple. It all comes down to this: if you make a good swing, you get a good shot; if you make a bad swing, you get a bad shot.

Many of the famous people I interviewed for this book said they found the golf course to be a refuge from daily life. It was no surprise that Jack felt the same way.

When I'm making a film, I'm very responsible. You give your life to it for a year, not just for the three months or however long you're filming. You're so specifically scheduled. I can't even read for fun while I'm working. That's half the reason I'm a bit of a nut. The other part of this life is that nobody talks to you who doesn't want something. I remember seeing Nick Price talking about the demands for his time when he was at the top of his game. I remember thinking, "Nick, do it for fifty years and see how you like it." That's why when I'm not working you can't make me schedule anything. If I didn't play golf, I wouldn't leave my house.

We talked about which players he admired most.

Tommy Bolt. Like my friend Rudy Durand said, there's only two things I need to work on: my short game and my temper. I've mellowed, but in the old days, if I hit a bad bunker shot, I'd fall on my back and pound my feet into the sand. I can relate to Tommy Bolt, and I really admire Jack Nicklaus. When he played in the British Open, I used to get his fan mail from Scotland. And Tiger, I mean, what can you say about him?

I couldn't resist asking him what his favorite golf film was.

The best sequence is in *Carefree* with Fred Astaire. He was an amazing athlete. He did everything well. In *Carefree* he does a dance routine where he hits five or six golf balls in a row, each perfectly. It's live, not processed. It's worth watching the film just for the sequence.

Finally, I asked him if there were any benefits to turning seventy.

I figure I've got one more shot at shooting my age.

. . .

In golf, as in life, you get out only as much as you put in, and that's the lesson I took away from my time with the tremendously private Jack Nicholson, who, while a star, isn't part of the Hollywood crowd. When he took up golf, he did so with a passion, and he worked very hard at becoming a good player. He brought the same single-minded dedica-

tion to the game that he brought to his acting, with many of the same successes. But when he cut back on practicing and playing, the results showed. Still, that hasn't diminished his love for the game. As he said, he was bitten twenty years ago and the effects haven't worn off yet.

As an aside, my conversation with Jack Nicholson reminded me of one I had with Jack Lemmon a year before he died. We had become friends over the years. He loved to talk about golf, and I loved to ask him about show business. We were on the driving range at Hillcrest Country Club, and he said he was hoping for one more chance to make the cut at Pebble Beach, which he had never done. He said that he had finally discovered the secret to golf: he just had to be himself.

"You have to be comfortable in your own skin," he said. "I've spent my life playing so many roles and being other people that I don't know who the real me is anymore. I think I would be a better golfer if I could find the real Jack Lemmon and sit down with him for a while. If I did that, I know my golf would improve."

Sadly, he didn't have enough time to find out. I'm just glad that I had the privilege of knowing him as long as I did.

LORENA OCHOA

I AM A BIG FAN of Lorena Ochoa. She is the real deal—the complete package. She obviously has an outstanding game, but what I most like about her is that for her, spirituality is not all about "me." She has her priorities in perfect order. Of course, golf (and winning) are important to her, but her family is very close-knit, and they come first in her life, followed by her foundation. Her wonderful, warm personality is one reason she's among the most popular players in golf today, male or female. While still in her twenties, she's already had a remarkable career.

Lorena grew up next door to the Guadalajara (Mexico) Country Club and took up the game at age five. She won her first state event the next year and her first national event at age seven. As a junior golfer, she won twenty-two state events in Guadalajara and forty-four national tournaments. She won five consecutive titles at the Junior World Golf Championships and enrolled in the University of Arizona in 2000. In

2001 and 2002, she won the NCAA Player of the Year Award, among many other awards. In her sophomore year, she won eight of the ten tournaments she entered and set an NCAA record by winning her first seven tournaments. In November 2001, Ochoa was presented with Mexico's National Sports Award by Mexican president Vicente Fox, the youngest winner of Mexico's most prestigious sports award. She left Arizona after her sophomore year, turned professional, and won three of the ten tournaments she entered on the 2002 Futures Tour, leading the money list and earning a spot on the LPGA Tour for the following season. In her first LPGA season, she was named the Louise Suggs Rolex Rookie of the Year, which I won in 1975, and the following year she won her first two tournaments. In 2006, she won six tournaments, led the LPGA's money list, and was named Player of the Year; she also won the Vare Trophy for lowest scoring average, and won the 2006 Associated Press Female Athlete of the Year Award. In April 2007, Ochoa overtook Annika Sorenstam to become the World's No. 1 female golfer. Later that year she won her first major championship, the Women's British Open, held at the Old Course at St. Andrews. She ended the season with winnings of more than $3 million, beating Sorenstam's previous record of $2,863,904. Ochoa also won the LPGA Rolex Player of the Year Award, led the money list, and was named the Women's Sports Foundation Sportswoman of the Year. She was just as impressive in 2008.

. . .

What is it about golf that attracted you to the game?

We lived next to the club, and I loved watching the pro hit balls, play, and practice. It just intrigued me. Both the mental and physical aspects appealed to me. I was one of four kids and we played a lot of other sports, but golf was always special for me. I'm a perfectionist. If I made a mistake with my homework, I'd start over. I'm also very competitive by nature. When I was young, the men at the club would let me play with them. I'd play from the back tees, which meant I wasn't hitting many greens, so I developed a good short game. I just loved the competition.

Did your family support you?

Absolutely. I was very lucky that my family supported me, both on and off the course. Girls rarely played golf in Mexico but my parents saw how happy it made me, so, yes, they supported me.

You said you're a very competitive person. How do you deal with losing? Does it take a lot out of you?

I hate to lose. I refuse to lose. The thing is that in golf you can lose in so many ways. You can make a bad swing or make a mistake in course management. I am very fortunate because I am an analytical person, so I can learn from my mistakes. I don't linger on defeats or mistakes. You can't be too hard on yourself. It doesn't accomplish anything. You just need to identify the mistake and fix it. It's like the 2006 U.S. Women's Open in Denver, when I hit the ball into the water. That hurt. It hurt a lot. But by the time I teed it up in the next tournament, I was ready to play.

You strike me as a very spiritual person. Is that right?

Yes. I was raised as a Catholic, and my spiritual life is very important to me. I pray every morning and night and try to attend Mass on Sundays. I think it's very important to keep a balanced life, and religion helps me do that. We have about twenty players on tour who belong to a religious group. It's nondenominational. All you have to believe in is Jesus Christ. It's where I can go to find peace and be with people who care about me as a person, not as a player. It's not about winning and losing golf tournaments. I've been very blessed. I have more than I could have ever imagined, but again, my faith helps me keep it all in perspective.

I know how all-consuming life on tour can be. Do you find yourself fighting against letting your career become too important?

When I turned pro, I signed with IMG [International Management Group], but it didn't work. They didn't understand my life, and I didn't want to change for them. I have to be happy outside of golf to play well. If I'm not happy, I can't play. My family will always be more important than my golf. We make decisions together. They may not always agree, but they're always there for me. That's one reason I still live in Mexico and have the same coach. It's worth the extra hours' flying so I can be with my family.

How long do you think you'll play on tour?

Not as long as people might think. Life is too short to do just one thing. I'd like to get married, have kids, and work on my foundation. We have an elementary school in Mexico, and I'd like to expand it so it is also a secondary school. We've given scholarships to kids and helped people with cancer. We also fund a program that matches organ donors with people who need transplants. In 2006, we helped with twenty transplants.

Whom do you admire?

I admire people who give back. I always try to learn positive things from people. I really admire my parents because they overcame hard times and were devoted to raising us. They are my heroes.

•　•　•

Lorena Ochoa is true to herself and, I think, an embodiment of the phrase *The truth will set you free.* I am also so impressed by her love for her family. They are the foundation upon which she built her success, and they provide the balance for her life today.

I remember reading something that the wonderful writer Calvin Trillin wrote about his late wife, Alice: ". . . we agreed on a simple notion: your children are either the center of your life or they're not, and the rest is commentary."

Lorena Ochoa is very lucky that her parents feel the same way.

DON OHLMEYER

B Y ANY STANDARD, Don Ohlmeyer ranks as one of the giants of the television industry.

He began his career as a gofer at ABC Sports, where he would go on to work on *Wide World of Sports*, produce *Monday Night Football*, and produce and direct three Olympics broadcasts. He moved to NBC Sports as executive producer, staying at the network from 1977 to 1982. He then formed his production company, Ohlmeyer Communications, which produced several made-for-television movies, network series, and specials. He won an Emmy for *Special Bulletin*, a 1983 television movie on nuclear terrorism.

Don returned to NBC in 1993 to become president of its West Coast division. At the time, the network was in third place in the ratings, but during his tenure there NBC returned to first place. He retired from NBC in 1999 and was then hired by ABC to revamp *Monday Night Football*, leaving after one season. He is currently a professor of television communications at Pepperdine University.

I had known Don from the outside looking in, beginning when he produced LPGA golf and then when I would see him at Bel-Air Country Club playing with his buddies. I would run into his son, Chris, who is a brilliant producer at ESPN, and ask about his dad. I was always hesitant to approach Don because he had an air of arrogance about him. I didn't think he liked me much, and he didn't seem to have much respect for women or for women's golf. That was my instinct, but after many years I decided to take a chance and approach him for an interview for my book. I'm glad I did. Don revealed his multidimensional personality and his many interests. He's a complex guy, yet very candid and open. During our conversation, we shared our experience of being close to—and molded by—our mothers. I was happy to find this common ground. As I was walking out the door of his house after the interview, I admitted that I'd always been a little scared of him. He put his arm around me and said, "It's nice to be in your book." We both laughed.

．　．　．

During my career I have known more than my share of competitive people, but I don't think I've ever met anyone quite as competitive as Don Ohlmeyer. We began our con-

versation at his home in Palm Desert, California, by talking about that aspect of his nature.

Whatever niceness and compassion I have I got from my dad, but the toughness that made me successful came from my mom, which is the reverse of what's normal. I was born in Cottonport, a little town in Louisiana, but we moved to the Chicago suburbs when I was a kid. My father was a great tennis player and started his own company, but he wasn't very successful. My mother was the head of physical education at a big high school and went on to become the first female athletic director in Illinois. She was a very tough person.

Were you close to your mother?

Not in the classic, close mother-child relationship. She drove me crazy. I was an only child. She did give me an understanding of what sports was all about, particularly women's sports. She knew women were getting screwed and I think she instilled that sense in me, but I wouldn't say I was on a mission to change things. It was more that I realized that women's sports were growing and it was a great opportunity. One of the first deals I did at NBC involved women's amateur sports. This was before the NCAA discovered that women even existed. We televised ten national championships. My mother was adamant that it was the best deal I ever did. Then, a few years later, I got

Ross Johnson, the head of Nabisco, to sponsor the LPGA's Dinah Shore tournament after Colgate dropped out.

Is your mother still alive?

No, she died about six months ago. It took me about six months to take her off my speed dial. I used to talk with her at least six times a week. Actually, she did most of the talking. I just listened.

Were you always interested in sports?

Mostly football, basketball, and baseball. I played baseball at Notre Dame and was the last freshman cut from the basketball team, but basically I've been involved in sports my whole life.

What about golf?

I played as a kid, but I was never really passionate about it. I don't think I played at all from 1967 until 1977. When I went to NBC, I began playing again, and then when I moved to Los Angeles I began playing three or four times a week.

Was it a social thing?

No. I love competition. My world has always been like a lifeboat. I've always understood that before someone gets in, someone else has to get out. I've never been really social. I try to be pleasant with people, but in my world I have friends and then I have acquaintances, and my friends are the people in the lifeboat and the acquaintances are the people in the water. I enjoy the camaraderie of golf. Some people are more fun to play with than others, but what I really enjoy is beating the hell out of somebody.

In that sense, do you think golf is like life?

I think all sports are, to some degree, but golf is very much like life. It teaches you to win gracefully and lose graciously. That's an important lesson to learn in life. Two of my sons play golf. They started at around age nine or ten. One son played on the Pepperdine University team that won the NCAAs in 1999. Golf has helped them relate to people, especially older people. It has also helped them because golf is a game of manners, honor, integrity, and sportsmanship. It's not like basketball, where people are jumping around pounding their chests and it's all me, me, me. There's humility in golf. All my kids have it, but I really see it in the two who play golf. Most kids you see who took up the game at an early age are well mannered. There are exceptions, of course, because there are obnoxious people in every walk of life. I met a twenty-two- or twenty-three-year-old kid a while ago who came to me for advice. After about five minutes I asked him if he'd played golf as a kid. He said he had, and he was now a 5-handicapper. I knew it just from the way he handled himself. You can see it. The other thing that golf does is teach you to not only play by the rules but to respect them. You don't see defensive backs in football calling pass interference on themselves or basketball players saying they traveled or goal-tended. In golf, you call penalties on yourself. I played golf the other day with a guy who called a double hit on himself. No one else could have seen it. That told me something about the guy.

Television has an artistic quality to it. Do you look at golf as a form of artistry?

In the execution, yes. You can know how to do something, but being able to do it under pressure is a completely different thing. It's what separates the really good players from the rest. And every time you try a difficult shot under pressure, you learn something about yourself, whether you pull it off or not. It's the same in my business. Lots of people talk about how to fix a problem, but the successful people are the ones that can actually solve it. That's why I knew Ohlmeyer Communications would be successful. I knew every aspect of the business and how to make it all work. The Skins Game was a perfect example.

In what way?

First of all, people told me I was nuts and that no one wanted to see four guys pretty much past their prime play a skins game if it wasn't for their own money. But I looked at it differently. First, I saw a pent-up demand for golf late in the year. Remember, back then the PGA Tour basically stopped playing tournaments after the World Series of Golf in late August. Second, in the early 1980s, the players on tour were perceived as mostly young, thin blond guys that no one knew anything about. But everyone knew Jack Nicklaus, Arnold Palmer, Gary Player, and Tom Watson. Did we take a chance? Sure. We had to cover all the production costs, sell all the commercial time, and pay NBC one million dollars. I'll tell you an interesting story about the first Skins Game. When I approached Jack [Nicklaus] about playing, one of the first questions he asked was if we were paying appearance fees. I hadn't even considered that. Jack said we absolutely shouldn't because if we did, people would think it was just an exhibition. I had always respected Jack, but that told me a lot about his character. One lesson I learned from Roone Arledge [the legendary head of ABC Sports and, later, ABC News] was to always listen to smart people, and I'm glad I listened to Jack. He was absolutely right. By not paying appearance fees, it gave the event credibility.

Is Jack still the greatest player you've ever seen?

Let me begin by saying that I've never seen any athlete who handles himself as well in every way—how he plays, presents himself, and handles the public—as Tiger Woods. As a player, he does things humans shouldn't even be allowed to do, and as a person, look how well he handles his life. You don't see stuff happening to him that happens to so many other professional athletes who become obsessed with themselves. I would say that Tiger, Arnold [Palmer], and Jack are the three greatest athletes I've ever seen. Jack surpassed Arnold in every aspect of his playing career except in the affection of the public. No one ever beat Arnold in that part of the game. But right now, I'd say Jack is still the greatest player who ever lived.

And Jack always remained true to himself. . . .

When he first came out on tour he was taciturn and even gruff, but that's how he needed to be to compete. I mean, you can look at his number of wins, which is amazing, especially in the majors, but the number of times he finished second is just as impressive. Still, Arnold had that quality of the guy next door that people loved—and still do.

Do you think there's too much money in golf right now?

I don't think the players think so. I know the women on the LPGA don't. But I wonder if it doesn't breed a certain complacency. People can earn so much money, both on and off the course, that they don't have to win. In a way, the Tour runs the risk of becoming like the NBA, where regular-season games don't matter, so guys just go through the motions. But having said that, the players with the real pride will always rise to the top. I give [PGA Tour commissioner] Tim Finchem and the Tour a lot of credit. They're playing for more money than anyone ever thought possible, and they've got corporations lined up to sponsor tournaments that don't make any sense from a marketing or advertising perspective, so they must be doing a lot of things right.

Didn't you play a role in the creation of the Champions Tour?

When I was at NBC, Fred Raphael, who had produced the old *Shell's Wonderful World of Golf,* came to me with the idea for the Legends of Golf events. I thought it was a great idea because it involved players people had actually heard of, like Sam Snead, Gene Sarazen, and Jimmy Demaret. Fred's problem was that he didn't have a sponsor and didn't have enough money. I wrote him a check, and the tournament was a huge success. A few years later, ten players led by Bob Goalby came to me with fifty thousand dollars they had raised among themselves and asked me to help start a senior tour. Deane Beman, then the commissioner of the PGA Tour, hadn't turned them down, but he wasn't really interested in starting or running their tour. We put together a package with Mazda that got their tour off the ground. Do you know what I'm proudest of in all that? The Champions Tour gave those guys fifty and older something to look forward to. They got in shape instead of sitting around a clubhouse drinking and smoking. It made me feel good to do something good for somebody else.

Were you very involved in the LPGA?

Not as much. If I could give one piece of advice to the LPGA and the people producing LPGA tournaments on television, it's this: people don't watch women's golf the way they watch the PGA Tour or even the Champions Tour. They like to see men struggle. That's why people love the Masters. But they like to see women succeed. That's the nature of our society. That's why when I was involved in the Nabisco Dinah Shore, I had them set up the [par-5] eighteenth hole so it was reachable in two. The fans and viewers loved it. They don't like to watch the women struggle like they do at the Women's Open, week after week. The LPGA should set up their courses so the players can make more birdies.

Has golf given much back to you?

In 1996 I went into rehab for drug and alcohol addiction. It was traumatic, but it was a great time for me. I recommend that everyone over forty spend thirty days really thinking about their lives. I had had a really successful career. I won a lot of awards and made a lot of money, but I realized that every time I'd become successful at one career, I'd become bored. Also, I realized that the price of success was missing out on a lot of things I wanted to do but couldn't because of my career. As a result, I was self-medicating. You can relate to that because of everything you had to give up so you could be successful in golf. People look at that life and think it's great and glamorous, but they don't see the sacrifices you had to make. It was the same with me. When I was in rehab, I realized that one of the things I missed was golf, so for the first three years after rehab, I played every day. I got down to a 3- or 4-handicap. My goal was to shoot a 69. Then I had colon surgery. One of the first questions I asked my doctor was how long I'd have to wait before I could begin playing. He said that I could start chipping in a week. Three weeks later, I shot a 69. A friend of mine said he was going to stop taking lessons and have colon surgery. The point is, my life is all about challenges. I never thought I could shoot 69, and after I did, I lost interest. That's just how I am. I just like the challenge that comes with setting your dreams and working to fulfill them—and then moving on to new dreams. People need to step out and take new risks. When I left NBC for the last time, I gave my replacement some advice: I told him he needed to have a burning desire to win, but he couldn't be interested in what's said about him in the press or at industry parties, since the two are mutually exclusive. Second, he needed to keep in mind that people don't really like you; they like the person who is sitting in that chair. That's how I approach golf and life. It's the curse of my mother.

.   .   .

When I think of Don Ohlmeyer, I think of the "Walter Hagen Lesson." Hagen was one of golf's greatest players, the winner of two U.S. Opens, four British Opens, and five PGA Championships, including four in a row from 1924 to 1927. Hagen was a great entertainer, both on and off the course, and once memorably observed that "life is short, so stop and smell the flowers along the way." That's a lesson that Don Ohlmeyer learned just in time, and it's a good lesson for all of us.

DONNA ORENDER

D ONNA ORENDER, who became president of the
Women's National Basketball Association in 2005,
is one of the most powerful women in sports. Growing up,
she was the ultimate tomboy, lettering in basketball, field
hockey, volleyball, softball, and tennis while in high school.
She was an All-American basketball player at Queens College, from which she graduated in 1978 with a degree in
psychology. She went on to graduate studies in social work
at Adelphi College. As Donna Geils (her maiden name),
she played for three seasons in the Women's Pro Basketball
League, and is one of just twenty women to have played in
all three years of the league's existence.

Donna began her television career as a production assistant at ABC Sports and went on to start her own production company, Primo Donna Productions. She spent
seventeen years at the PGA Tour, eventually becoming the
senior vice president of strategic development in 2001. The

original producer of *Inside the PGA Tour,* she was a key member of the team that negotiated the Tour's television contracts. In 2005 she left the Tour to become president of the WNBA. Donna is married to M. G. Orender, a former executive with the PGA of America and golf course developer, and they have two sons, Zachary and Jacob.

. . .

Since Donna was actively competing in sports before the full effects of Title IX legislation (which mandated equal opportunities and funding for female collegiate athletes) were felt, I asked her about sports when she was growing up.

I liked all sports, but tennis was really my first love. My father played soccer, and sports were always part of my environment. I grew up in a typical Jewish household on Long Island. My father always stressed that I should do my best, whatever I was doing. My mother was very proactive. To be honest, though, neither of them really felt sports were the place for their daughter to be. It took a long time for them to get there.

Do you think that young women who are raised around sports, especially team sports, have more self-esteem and are better suited to dealing with life as adults?

Without a doubt. I believe that sports are a game changer for girls, just as they've always been for boys. I think if a woman grows up playing sports, it teaches lessons like self-reliance and teamwork. I feel very strongly that sports help level the playing field between men and women. There's no doubt in my mind that's true.

You've been involved with sports in television, then on the Tour, and now at the WNBA. Sports and television have traditionally been male dominated. Are there pluses and minuses to being a woman in those worlds?

Because I was an athlete and had succeeded at the highest level of my sport, I always felt supremely confident in those environments. I understood sports and I understood teamwork. If I had worked on Wall Street, it might have been a different story, because that's not an environment I would have been as comfortable in—although as a competitive person I would have done pretty well, I think. But in sports I've never felt intimidated. I can go into meetings with Billy Packer or Dean Smith or anyone in basketball and know that no one loves the game more than I do. Was I aware of how women are treated in sports and television? Sure. But I was never intimidated. Plus, when I was at ABC, I started as a production assistant, which basically means you do a lot of gofer jobs. I paid my dues and learned the business from the bottom up, so I think people in the business respected that.

Let's talk about golf. How's your game?

I didn't take up golf full-time until I went to the Tour. Of course, my husband is very active in the golf business, so I'm always in a golf environment. As for my game, it seems like I always fight going out to play, mostly because I just don't have the time. But once I do get out there, I'm supremely grateful for the chance to be playing. It usually takes me a couple of holes to slow down and detox. I really am enthusiastic once I'm out there, but my kids tease me that I think grocery shopping is a great experience, so I guess that's just my nature. I just love the natural setting and social aspects of the game. I'm at the point in my life, because my schedule is so hectic, that my favorite people to play with are my husband and kids. We're a pretty competitive group.

As a competitor, you know the value of preparation. . . .

I love the concept but I don't have time to prepare. I usually hit a couple of drives on the practice range and then go. It's like I play ADD [attention deficit disorder] golf. If I was going to play competitively it would be a different story, but I'm just out there to have some fun.

Did your basketball career carry over to your golf game?

I think so. I try to hold on to the wonder of a good shot. In golf, it's very easy to focus on the bad ones. You can't hold on to the negativity. Each shot is an individual shot, just like in basketball. I also try to remember to take in the serenity offered by a golf course.

In all the time you were involved with golf, did you ever get a tip that really worked for you?

I did all these videos and taped segments. I got tips from everyone, all the best players in the world. The best one was from Jack Nicklaus. He said when you're putting, always point the logo of the ball on the line you want to start the ball. He said that helps you align yourself properly. As an athlete, I always had trouble aligning my body, so that stuck with me.

Do you have a favorite course?

I have some favorite experiences at certain courses. I did a documentary on the Old Course at St. Andrews, so that will always be a special place for me. I played Pebble Beach with my husband when we were first dating each other, so that will always be special. I made three pars at Augusta National the first time I played it. Those are all special experiences for me.

You were at the PGA Tour for seventeen years. That's a long time. Do you miss it?

In a way, the people there are like family and friends, and in some ways I don't feel that I'm away from it. Really, though, I just closed one door and opened another.

What is a real "wow" for you?

Being able to elevate the WNBA to the next level, and we're on the right path; but a much larger "wow" would be helping to raise the self-esteem and awareness of women. That's an important change because it is central to how women are viewed and how we view ourselves. Sport is a cultural, emotional, and business currency, and I want to help women understand that and buy into it.

. . .

Donna Orender has succeeded because of her willingness to pursue her dreams—in this case, playing basketball at the highest levels of the game and then combining her passion for sports with a successful career while raising a family. But just as important is her willingness to use her position of influence as president of the WNBA to improve the lives of women, both today and for generations to come. All of us can help make changes, and some of those changes are larger than others. But it's the importance of caring and stepping up to the challenge that makes Donna a special person in my eyes.

DOTTIE PEPPER

DOTTIE PEPPER joined the LPGA Tour in 1988, and right from the first I recognized that she had not only the game to win but the attitude and determination to make it happen.

I'm going to let you in on a little secret: there are plenty of players out there—professional and amateur—who have the talent to win but they just aren't comfortable when they get in a position to do the job. My teacher, Walter Keller, recognized this, and when I began to compete in junior tournaments in Southern California, he told me something that has stuck with me ever since.

"Amy," he said, "if you want everyone to like you, finish fifteenth."

I can tell you right now that Dottie Pepper has never really cared that much if everyone likes her. In fact, she's a good person to have on your side in a fight. She wanted to win, and she was feisty enough and talented enough to pull it off. I respect her overall game, but what I really admire about her is that she *wanted* and *knew how* to win. That was especially true in match play, where she excelled.

The proof is in the history books. She won seventeen times on our tour, including two major championships, and played on six United States Solheim Cup teams. She was the Rolex Player of the Year in 1992, the same year that she won the Vare Trophy for low scoring average, and was our leading money winner.

Another thing I like about Dottie is that she never concealed her emotions. When things were going her way, the joy was there for everyone to share. And when she didn't hit a shot the way she expected, she wasn't shy about letting her frustration show with a slap of her thigh . . . or something even more demonstrative. She reminded me of one of my idols, Babe Zaharias, in her sheer bravado, or of my friend Patty Sheehan, who loved nothing better than to spring into a series of cartwheels to celebrate a win.

Dottie is best known today for her work as a golf announcer for NBC, The Golf Channel, and ESPN. She turned to broadcasting after a series of back and wrist injuries forced her to retire from competitive golf at the end of the 2004 season.

We sat down at the clubhouse at the Bighorn Golf Club in Palm Desert, where she was broadcasting the 2006 Samsung World Championship for NBC. Dottie has mellowed a bit (but just a bit) since her playing days, but the passion and intensity are still there. She's just focused them on her new career. We began by talking about how she got started playing golf.

. . .

I grew up on a turkey farm in Saratoga Springs, New York, and sports were always a big part of my life. My father, Don, was a first baseman for the Detroit Tigers, and my mother's family owned a ski shop and had an interest in a local ski area. My maternal grandmother was the golfer in the family, and she got me started by giving me a series of lessons when I was about to turn eight. She was one of thirteen children whose parents emigrated from Germany. She was kind of a stern, staunch woman. She was very tough, but she was a golfer. It's funny, but I'm kind of the reverse of Phil Mickelson. My father is a righty in everything except golf. The only thing he did as a lefty was bat and play golf, and I developed my swing by trying to mirror his.

I always knew I wanted to play on the LPGA Tour, but skipping college was never an option in my family. Education was very important. I went to Furman and had a great time. I think college is really important because as an athlete, there's always the possibility of a career-ending injury, or you might just fall out of love with what you're doing.

Our conversation turned to the psychology of winning, and she gave me an insight into her determination and attention to detail.

In my golf library at home, I have a small, old book written by Sam Snead. The pages are yellowed and literally held together by gobs of glue. Sam wrote about how important it is to take every advantage you can, no matter how small. Sam wrote that in head-to-head matches, he noticed that when players became nervous or uncomfortable, something would change in their game. Maybe it was their preshot routine or how much time they took over the ball. He told a story about playing Ben Hogan in a playoff for the 1954 Masters. On the par-3 sixteenth, he noticed that Hogan smoked an entire cigarette while preparing to putt. Sam took that as a sign that the pressure was getting to Ben, and that boosted his confidence. He made an aggressive approach putt, trying to turn up the heat on Hogan. It worked. Hogan three-putted and Sam went on to win by a stroke, 71 to 72. That was a lesson I really took to heart, and it's helped me many times.

As Dottie told me that story, I realized it was her attention to detail that had led her to be so disciplined in her thinking. That same attention to detail became evident when she discussed her decision to retire from competition—a decision that had to be incredibly painful because mentally she was still capable of winning. It was her body that finally let her down. Retirement revealed a softer side, which was evident when she spoke about her dog, a chow.

The year I came back from my first shoulder surgery, I was paired with Michael Chang, the 1989 French Open tennis champion, in the pro-am at the Nabisco Dinah Shore. He was at a crossroads in his life and career, spending more time searching his soul than working on the tennis court. He said he had reached the point of diminishing returns, putting more into the game than he was getting out of it. He said he just didn't feel he could do enough to get where he wanted to be in the game. Later that summer, I had my own "uh-oh, we're here" moment when I had to face the "big question mark." I was filled with uncertainty, but not fear. I mean, when I was playing, my career was all-encompassing, and then I realized, "It's gone."

Dottie and I spoke about the difficulty of winding down a competitive career, and we agreed that for both of us—and for most successful professionals—the course is not only our stage but our sanctuary. In fact, for some people who are very competitive, it's a way to overcome or mask insecurities.

It's a time-out, a safe place, no question. I will tell you that after I got divorced for the first time, rounds of golf never went faster. I mean, literally, I'm already on the sixteenth hole? You're kidding. That's one way golf is like life. You only get out of it what you put in, and if you're going to wallow around in your problems, you're not going to get much out of it. I gave it my all and got a whole lot out of it.

Once Dottie made the transition to a television career, it soon became obvious that she was a natural—although, as a "natural" golfer knows, it doesn't mean there's no hard work or preparation involved.

Judy Rankin encouraged me and was very helpful right from the beginning, and it all shook itself out relatively quickly. I learned early on that, just like golf, you have to spend a lot more time preparing than you do playing the course or during a broadcast. It makes your job easier because there aren't as many surprises, and it's more fun. I was very impressed by how hard [ABC and ESPN golf anchor] Mike Tirico worked at preparing for a telecast, and I look forward to the advice I still get from him here and there. He's been a great role model.

I asked Dottie if she had any long-term goals or planned just to approach life as it came.

Right now I have a six-year plan because I just signed a six-year contract, so that's the window I'm committed to. But just as I didn't want to play forever, I don't want to do this forever, because I think there's just so much more to do in life. But for right now, I'm having a heck of a time doing it . . . a really good time!

· · ·

When I look at Dottie, I'm impressed by her career and her accomplishments, but what strikes me more is her willingness to accept the fact that nothing in this life lasts forever and change is always lurking right around the corner. Dottie accepted that change with the same passion and determination that brought about her success on the golf course. She looks at change as a challenge and a gift, and she has embraced it. We can all learn from that.

KYRA PHILLIPS

M Y FRIEND KYRA PHILLIPS anchors the afternoon edition of *CNN Newsroom,* but she's every bit as comfortable outside the studio as behind the anchor desk. She has covered an amazing variety of events, including the Atlanta courthouse shooting, Hurricane Katrina from New Orleans in 2005, and the Iraq war, and she participated in CNN's 2000 and 2002 election coverage. Kyra also covered the September 11 terrorist attacks. In January 2002, she spent a month on location in Antarctica, working on a documentary, and that same year she became the first female journalist to fly in an F-14 air-to-air combat training mission over the Persian Gulf.

My kind of girl!

I first met Kyra when she was working as an investigative reporter in the Special Assignment Unit for KCBS-TV in Los Angeles. Over the years she's won four Emmy Awards and two Edward R. Murrow Awards for investigative reporting, and the Associated Press named her Reporter of the Year in 1997.

If that weren't enough, she's actively involved in charities like the Big Brothers/Big Sisters of America mentoring program and is on the board of the Brain Tumor Foundation for Children. Each year she hosts a tournament at Chateau Elan Golf Club near Atlanta to raise money for research into brain tumors, which caused the death of her grandfather.

We began our conversation by talking about her grandfather.

.   .   .

My mother was a single mom, so he was everything to me—a mentor, my best friend, everything. The day I was born, he won his flight for the club championship at Jacksonville Country Club in Illinois. He was at the hospital when I was born. He said it was the greatest day of his life. He put a golf club in my hands when I was two. When I was little we'd go to the golf course and he'd pull me around on his golf cart. I took him to the Masters one year. He looked around and said, "Ah, I've lived." After he died I scattered his ashes at the thirteenth hole, the "Azalea" hole.

I know that after he died you went through a difficult period.

It's funny how things sometimes come together spiritually in your life. I was devastated when my grandpa died. I couldn't sleep. I couldn't read. One night when I was really down I was watching Larry King, and Deepak Chopra was his guest. He was talking about life after death. What he was saying really resonated with me. Right after that, one of our bookers called and asked if I was interested in having Deepak on. I met him off the air and told him about my grandfather. I was sobbing. He comforted me and told me I was going to be okay. The next day, all his books and CDs arrived. It was a very moving experience, and it helped me stay spiritually intact.

You've had so many amazing experiences in your career, flying jets and traveling to dangerous places all over the world. Golf must seem pretty tame.

I am a thrill seeker, I admit. But I love golf because it's a constant challenge. I try to play wherever I can. The game frustrates me because I can't become more consistent. I used to be a six but not anymore. I think it's the challenge that keeps me coming back. The game is so complicated and spiritual for me. I love the beautiful places it takes me. I like the quiet, but I also like it because it helps me bond with people. It's really the last remaining classy sport.

Do you have a round that was special?

Not one particular round. I remember certain times that were just so much fun. There was so much laughter. For me, it's just a perfect escape from everything.

You said that golf helps you bond with people. Has it helped you in your career?

It has really helped me win men over. If you can play golf, you relate better. It's helped me with admirals and generals because it helps you establish a relationship based on trust. I remember working a piece about the air force's response right after 9/11. The trust I had with some of the generals made the piece possible.

Have you interviewed many golfers over the years?

Sure. Phil Mickelson, Annika, Chris DiMarco, Retief Goosen. I remember interviewing you about Augusta National's policy on admitting women members. The day Payne Stewart died in a plane crash I was anchoring the afternoon program on CNN for the first time. I had interviewed Payne in the past, and I knew a lot about airplanes. It was just strange that it happened on my first day anchoring.

Is there any place you haven't played that you'd like to play?

Ireland, definitely. My grandpa was Irish, so it would be very special for me.

What about a person to play with?

Bobby Jones. He fascinates me. He was so elegant and had so much humility. He was extremely intelligent, and his courage in the last part of his life is so inspirational.

Anyone else?

Jesus Christ, I'd like to see if he'd take a mulligan. What would Jesus do? That's the question. And maybe Kenny Chesney. I've always liked his music. Maybe it's the country girl in me.

·   ·   ·

Kyra has always grabbed life by the horns, which for me is the only way to experience life. She has also tempered that drive by being a woman who steadfastly seeks her own truth. Through good and bad, her resiliency and curiosity have always seen her through—good lessons in staying on top of your game in golf and in life.

REX PICKETT

R EX PICKETT is one of those classic "overnight success" stories—but only if your definition of overnight is about twenty years.

Rex, now fifty-five, grew up in San Diego and, after graduating from the University of California, San Diego, enjoyed some early success as a screenwriter. But by the late 1990s, his life was pretty much in shambles. His marriage had dissolved, he was basically broke, and his writing was going nowhere fast. When he looked in the rearview mirror of his life, he didn't like what he saw, and the view down the road didn't hold much promise, either.

In 1998 Pickett followed the advice every writer has heard a hundred times: write what you know. What he knew best was the story of his life as a struggling writer trying to overcome his divorce from a woman he still cared about and respected. The story took the main character north from Los Angeles to the wine country in California's central coastal region, where he and his best friend—a good-natured womanizer trying to come to grips with his impending marriage—indulged in a road trip of wine, women, and golf . . . pretty much in that order of importance.

The novel had been rejected by twelve publishers when, by a happy accident of fate, his agent sent it to director Alexander Payne, who liked the story and optioned it for $12,500. At about the same time, St. Martin's Press agreed to pay Pickett a $5,000 advance.

The movie based on the book was *Sideways,* which received five Oscar nominations, won one for Best Adapted Screenplay, and was the most honored film of 2004.

The film's success altered Pickett's life forever, mostly for the better. But, as he revealed during the course of our long conversation at Riviera Country Club, success can be a double-edged sword.

. . .

We began by talking about how he got started in writing and in golf.

My father was in the air force. During World War II he flew over the Hump, from India to China over the Himalayas. It was incredibly dangerous. More crews were lost flying over the Hump than over Europe. He stayed in the air force after the war, and then he left the service when he was in his thirties and we moved to San Diego, where he got into the laundry business. We were pretty middle-class, but we did join Stardust Country Club [now Riverwalk Country Club], and I started playing golf there when I was about eight or nine. Actually, the first course I ever played on was Torrey Pines North. It was so beautiful. I just got hooked on the game. I rarely practiced. I just liked playing, and by the time I was twelve, I was playing in the thirteen-to-fourteen-year-old division of the San Diego Junior Golf Association and was even beating sixteen- and seventeen-year-olds. There were a lot of really good golfers that came out of San Diego.

My two brothers played, too, but we never had very good equipment. My father was a little on the cheap side. I remember a kid named Aly Trompas. There were a lot of good golfers in his family. Aly used to take lessons from Gene Littler. I remember that Aly had a Bulls Eye putter that I coveted. I quit golf at age fourteen, and being a little self-conscious about money may have had something to do with it. At the time, though, there was a lot of peer pressure about playing golf. If you played, people thought you were a sissy. Besides, I had started surfing. It's interesting that I chose two sports that you could do by yourself. I've never been very interested in team sports.

When I was seventeen, I was bitten by the writing bug. I wrote a poem for my high school [Claremont High School] about the principal, and it caused a stir. I studied writing and film at UCSD, and that's where I met my future wife. We made two films together. One was bought by German television and the other by Island Films, and they never went anywhere.

So far, it sounded like life was treating Rex pretty well. Then he began to explain what went wrong.

In the early 1990s, my agent died from AIDS, my mother had a massive stroke, and my wife and I broke up. She moved to New York to study at the American Film Institute. We remain friends, and we even collaborated on a short film, *My Mother Dreams the Satan's Disciples in New York*, which won an Oscar. She directed and I wrote the screenplay. But again, by the early 90s, things were pretty bad. I would have been happy working as a barista at Starbucks. If I could have afforded a gun, I would have killed myself.

People cared about me and I had a few writing jobs, but it was about this time that golf saved me. I wanted to play but I couldn't afford the courses around Los Angeles, so I used to play at the old Malibu Country Club, which is a really nice Billy Bell course. The problem was, it had been taken over by a religious organization, the Church of Perfect Liberty. So I headed up to Santa Barbara and played Sandpiper, which I loved. Then someone told me I should go over the hill to Lompoc. I played La Purisima and Hunter Ranch and fell in love with the area. I had a special feeling for La Puri-sima, which was designed by Robert Muir Graves. I could go there in the middle of the week and just go out by my-self. It's a great course in great condition, and there are no houses on it. It's a very unpopulated area. I began to spend a lot of time up there. On one trip, a friend of mine came up for a couple of days. That was the basis of *Sideways*. When *Sideways* became successful and I'd earned enough money to become really comfortable, I thought the ideal life would be to move to Lompoc, write in the morning, and then play golf in the afternoon. Then I realized I'd go mad.

Since I've always viewed golf as a form of artistic expres-sion, I wondered how Rex related golf to writing.

They're alike in a lot of different ways. First of all, there's a discipline involved in both. When I was learning to play as a kid, one of the things that really stuck with me is that every single shot counts. You can't afford to be sloppy. The same is true with writing. Every word, every sentence, every para-graph has to be as good as you can make it. Every word counts. You can't screw around. It's just like on the golf course.

Writing, like any art, is about attention to form. It's about the craft. Golf and writing are both journeys, and I look at life that way. I'm on the back nine of life, but then, on most courses, the holes on the back nine are usually a lot more interesting than those on the front. Also, every hole is different every day.

The winds change. The holes and tee positions change. The weather changes. It's like life that way. Every day is different. It's like personal relationships. They're always changing, too.

I think writing and golf are also alike in that you have to be honest with yourself. I can go out there by myself and if I miss a two-footer, my conscience tells me that someone is watching. The people in the movie industry that I play with are all cheaters. I played with a very prominent producer one day. We came off the eighteenth green and he announced that he was buying lunch because he had finally broken 90. He hadn't come close, and by saying he had, he was doing a disservice to himself and to the guy who did shoot an 89.

I also like golf because once I'm on the course, all the stresses seem to effervesce. It's just club, ball, and hole. I can completely lose myself to the real world. At the same time, I like knowing that I can play golf with people I have nothing in common with except golf and still have a good time. I can find a commonality that I might not find in any other setting.

I guess the last way golf and writing and life are alike is that when I finally get to the eighteenth hole, there's a sense of relief.

I asked Rex if he'd be nervous or excited if he had a chance to shoot his best round.

Scared. Really scared. A few months ago I played Riviera with John Atwood, the editor of *Travel & Leisure Golf.*

The Santa Ana winds were really blowing, but I birdied one and five and was 1-under through five. I knew there was no way that was going to keep up—and it didn't. It's all about getting into the zone. One day in the early 1990s, when I was totally broke, I went to the Hitching Post [the restaurant featured in *Sideways*, where Rex has a lifetime pass for free dining, thanks to the publicity the restaurant received from the movie] and had about nine Pinots. When the alarm clock went off the next morning at five, I had to check my driver's license to see what my name was. We played La Purisima from the back tees and I was 1-under through twelve with an unbelievable hangover. But I was in the zone. You look at someone like Hilary Lunke, who won the 2003 Women's Open in a playoff. I mean, she hung in there for ninety holes, but she hasn't done anything since. Not to take anything away from her, but that's a perfect case of getting in the zone. Or you look at Rick Rhoden. Great pitcher who has won a lot of celebrity golf events, but when he tries to qualify for the Champions Tour, the edge isn't there. He can shoot 70, 71 at home all week, but if he tries to qualify, it's not there.

I asked him if there was a golf course he'd like to play or a person he'd like to play with.

Cypress Point, because it seems fair. I don't like courses that cripple people. As for a golfer, I don't have any great desire to play with professional golfers. They don't seem that interesting. I wonder if hitting that many golf balls has reduced their number of brain cells.

Since Sideways *is at least partly autobiographical, I asked Rex what he thought about Paul Giamatti, who played him in the movie.*

Once I got past the fact that he was bald and had hair on his back, I was fine. He did a great job. He has so much soul and so much heart.

Finally, I asked him if success had changed his life.

Success is hard, at least for me. Imagine that you had dropped off the face of the planet and then you're suddenly successful and everyone wants a piece of you—wine festivals, cruise ships. When I wrote the book, I had everything to gain and nothing to lose, like when I shot that round after nine Pinots. I had nothing to lose. There was no pressure. Now I have everything to lose every time I turn on the computer. Success doesn't help me write the next page. It's made writing harder. I've already had to get a couple of extensions on my next novel.

Success does not produce the next great page, just like it doesn't produce the next great drive under pressure. All the success and the money does is get you into the last group. Then it's up to you to perform.

．　．　．

People always say that success breeds success, but that isn't always true. It breeds success only if you can come to grips with the pressures you're going to face. When I was playing my best golf, I approached the first tee of a tournament *confident* that I could win because I had won at every level of competition and therefore understood those expectations and that pressure. When my competitive career wound down, I no longer felt that way. The edge was off, and I knew it. For Rex, success came late in life, after struggling for so many years, and that can be difficult to keep in perspective. It's like one of the final scenes from the film *The Candidate*, starring Robert Redford as a young idealist who runs for the United States Senate. Against all the odds, and having compromised his beliefs, he wins. At the moment of his victory, he asks a friend, "Now what?"

That's the million-dollar question that comes with success.

DENNIS QUAID

THE LONGER I'M AROUND GOLF, the more I've come to realize that there are a lot of people who can talk a good game and a lot fewer who can actually play a good game. Actor Dennis Quaid is someone who can play a good game. He has a legitimate handicap of 6 at Bel-Air, which is no small accomplishment.

Dennis, age forty-four, grew up in Houston and attended the University of Houston. In 1974, after some success in amateur productions, he joined his older brother, Randy, in Los Angeles. Randy had already established himself as an actor, and it wasn't long before Dennis did as well, making his film debut in 1977 in *9/30/55*.

In the years since, he has appeared in many films, including *Breaking Away*, *The Long Riders* (with his brother, Randy), *The Right Stuff*, and *Wyatt Earp*, and is currently enjoying a great run.

In 1998 Dennis took a leave from his career and went

into rehab to break his addiction to cocaine. He very candidly began our conversation by discussing his experience
in rehab and how it led to his love of golf.

. . .

By the time I was in my late thirties I was seriously addicted to cocaine, and I knew I wasn't going to be able
to shake it by myself, so I went into a clinic. I was thirty-
eight years old. When I got out of the clinic—actually the
day I got out—I took up golf with a passion. I had played
sporadically before, but it never held my interest. My
father, Buddy, loved golf. He was an electrician and had
a 1-handicap. He always tried to get me involved in the
game, but I couldn't see the fascination. For some reason,
after rehab, I could.

*When I spoke with Dennis Hopper, I learned that he had
an almost identical experience. He went into rehab, and
when he came out he immediately fell in love with golf. It
was like he replaced one addiction with another—although
one is a lot healthier for you.*

For me, it was interesting because rehab helped me understand that if you're honest with yourself, golf will reveal
your true personality and character. People say golf builds
character. Maybe, but I think it actually reveals character.
I think whatever is inside you will come out on the golf

course. In my case, golf taught me that I have to learn to be patient and not get too greedy. If you get too greedy in this game, you don't have a chance. I think life is a lot like that.

What do you like most about golf?

Everything. I like to just be out on beautiful courses. I mean, my favorite courses are Pebble Beach, the Old Course at St. Andrews, and the National Golf Links, but I could be happy just walking them and not hitting a single shot. I like to practice, because for me, it's a kind of meditation. You can get out of your head and into a zone. I like just going out and playing with my friends. And I like to take lessons. Eddie Merrins was my first teacher. I've worked with Butch Harmon and a few others. I tend to get the information and then move along to someone new.

What's your best round?

I had a 70 at Barton Creek [in Austin], and I knew exactly where I was in terms of score throughout the round. It was a very, very easy round and I felt as though I had arrived.

Does your experience as an actor help you in golf?

It's interesting, because as an actor you learn all the technique and then just forget it and let the Acting Gods take over. In the end, you're not hired to play a role as much as you're hired to be what they think you are. It's the same in golf. You learn the technique and then try to let the Golf Gods go to work.

You had a lot of success in films, making a lot of movies all at once, and then it kind of fell off. What did that teach you?

I've come to accept that life is a series of peaks and valleys and you have to try to keep things, both good and bad, in perspective. Making movies is just like that, and so is golf. Sometimes you just don't really know where you are. You'll be playing great and then it will just disappear and you wonder if you'll ever play well again.

This is a two-part question: the first part is, why aren't there more good golf movies? And the second is, would you have liked to play Kevin Costner's role in Tin Cup?

One reason there are so few good golf movies is that studios cast guys who can't play golf in the lead roles. You can fake a lot of things in movies, but you can't fake a good golf swing. As for *Tin Cup,* I would have loved that role but it didn't happen. I've got a project for a golf film I'm working on now, and I think we have a good chance of getting it made.

You said that your father tried to interest you in the game when you were a kid. Have you tried to introduce your son, Jack Henry, to golf?

He's fifteen. I've tried to expose him to golf but not force the game on him. He's like me. He's into drama and girls.

If you had been good enough, would you have liked being a Tour pro?

Everyone has dreams of playing the Tour, but you have to weigh reality. First of all, you'd have to be a lot better player than I am or ever was. Besides, I couldn't take the week-in-and-week-out grind. I like my life just the way it is today. I take my son to school, then play golf, and then ride my horse up through Will Rogers State Park. It's a very nice life.

· · ·

When I think about Dennis Quaid, I realize how important it is to find a sense of tranquillity and perspective in life. In America, we put a huge emphasis on success—but success can come at a very high price. It's crucial to have a space in your life where nothing bothers you and you can find a sense of inner peace. Golf has helped Dennis Quaid do just that.

PAM SHRIVER

P AM SHRIVER is Maryland born and bred but she lives in Los Angeles. I had seen her around Santa Monica and at Riviera, but I didn't really get to know her until we sat down to talk at her house in Brentwood.

During the 1980s and 1990s, she was one of the top women tennis players in the world, winning 133 professional events, including 22 women's doubles titles and one mixed-doubles title, in Grand Slam tournaments. She also teamed with Zina Garrison to win a women's doubles gold medal at the 1988 Olympic Games in Seoul, South Korea. I first became aware of Pam Shriver during the 1978 U.S. Open, in which, as an unseeded sixteen-year-old amateur, she reached the women's singles final Open. On her way to the final she defeated Wimbledon champion Martina Navratilova in a dramatic semifinal, 7–6, 7–6. The fairy tale ended when she lost to Chris Evert in the final, 7–5, 6–4. That was the only Grand Slam final she reached, however, as she ran into stiff competition in the next eight semi-finals, losing four to Navratilova, two to Steffi Graf, and one each to Evert and Hana Mandlikova.

In 1978 she teamed with Navratilova in a formidable doubles partnership. They won seven Australian Open, five French Open, five Wimbledon, and four U.S. Open titles. In 1984, the pair captured all four Grand Slam women's doubles titles, which was part of a record 109-match winning streak between 1983 and 1985. She also won the 1987 French mixed-doubles title with Emilio Sanchez. She is one of only five female players in the Open era to have won more than one hundred career titles.

Following the end of her playing career in 1996, Shriver mentored Venus Williams and went on to work as a commentator for ABC, CBS, ESPN, the BBC, and 7 Sport in Australia. She served as president of the WTA Tour Players Association from 1991 to 1994 and has been president of the USA Tennis Foundation and on the board of directors of the United States Tennis Association. She was inducted into the International Tennis Hall of Fame in 2002.

Pam's first husband, Joe Shapiro, a former Walt Disney Company lawyer, died of non-Hodgkin's lymphoma in 1999, and three years later she married George Lazenby, an actor best known for his performance as James Bond in *On Her Majesty's Secret Service*. They have three children, George Jr. and twins Kate and Sam.

Pam is the women's golf champion at Brentwood Country Club, so I began our interview by asking if her tennis skills carried over to golf.

. . .

I never really played very much until I retired from competition. If I was at a nice resort like Hilton Head or Greenlefe, I might play two or three times a year, and I played when we took family vacations at Kapalua. I enjoyed it, but as a tennis player I thought it should be an easy game because you're hitting a stationary object. That was before I realized the hitting area was tiny and the errors are so magnified. The more I played, the more I realized how difficult golf is, and I liked the challenge. It's a funny thing: Martina is a lefty but she plays golf right-handed. Rod Laver is the same, but Ken Rosewall is a righty who plays golf left-handed. They all had great backhands. Maybe there's something to that. Maybe I should try playing as a lefty.

What's the strength of your golf game?

I'm not that long, so I have to be really accurate. I have a short game that's scary good, which I think has something to do with seeing the angles in tennis. I'm a streaky putter. When I can feel the speed, I'm pretty good.

What's the best tip you ever received?

My late husband, Joe, told me to trust my athletic ability. I never learned a proper grip, and I'm probably not going to because I'm not doing this to be a pro. It works. Because I'm tall and have a good build, I think if I had focused on golf I could have been really good, maybe as good as I was in tennis.

You must have had a preshot routine when you served in tennis. Do you have one for golf?

I'm a big believer in rituals. Before I hit a shot, I stand behind the ball and hold the club like a rifle. I pick a spot to shoot at. It has something to do with your master eye. My dad loved to hunt, particularly game birds. It probably carried over from that. I use the club like a scope. I know hunting isn't all that politically correct, but it was a big part of our lives. He'd go out and shoot on Chesapeake Bay, and we'd have these wonderful duck dinners. I think if you eat what you shoot, it's fine.

You were very close to your dad. . . .

I lost my older sister and my first husband to cancer, and then I lost my father. It happened at a point in my life when I had settled into a routine. I was headed towards retirement from tennis. I was living in a familiar place with constant friends and I was very much set in my ways. All of a sudden there was this shock and grief, and it changes the path of your life. Golf helped me get through all that. I think any activity helps you get through great stress, but golf is especially good. It's very peaceful.

When did you know it was time to retire from tennis?

It's a funny thing. I was a tomboy when I was a kid and just loved to compete, but sometimes the stress of competition got to be too much for me, even early on. I remember playing in the sixteen-and-unders in the club championship. All of a sudden I couldn't breathe. I had to sit down on the court and try to get some air. The ninety-degree humidity of Baltimore in August might have had something to do with it, but I doubt it.

Sometimes athletes appear ironclad to the public. . . .

That's usually self-imposed. I remember one day, it was about eight years after I had been a pro, I made a toss for a serve and it went haywire. It's like a yip in golf. It just came out of the blue. I thought, "Where did that come from?" When it happened later at Wimbledon it was like a warning. Basically, my quality singles play ended in the early 1990s. I was fortunate that I had a lot of success in doubles.

Does golf fulfill your need to be competitive?

I love playing. The social aspect is so different from tennis, where the only time you speak to your opponent is during end changes and before and after a match. In golf, you can talk all the time.

Martina was your great doubles partner. Do you ever play golf together?

We have a ball. She is such a great athlete and so competitive, plus she's fun to play with because she's so smart and funny. I remember the first time she played with George [Pam's husband] and me at Brentwood. She hit her drive on the first hole into the trees. This guy yelled, "It's a good thing you're a tennis player." She gave him the finger.

How's your game today?

I'm a 5 but I'm not consistent. I have so much going on, and I want to do everything so well—I have three kids, and I manage the house. Plus I have my television work to think of. The twins were born two months early, and I took time off from broadcasting to be with them. When I came back, I had gone from being a commentator to doing on-court reporting. I didn't think that was right, so I raised the issue, and that made some network people squirm. Did it close some doors? We'll see.

If you had an ideal foursome, who would it include?

Bill and Melinda Gates. I find philanthropy a really fascinating topic, and here are two people who are literally trying to change the world. I like funny people, so maybe Johnny Carson, although he might be too funny. I couldn't concentrate. Maybe Lucille Ball and Carol Burnett . . . no, they might be too competitive.

.   .   .

Pam Shriver has enjoyed several careers. First, she was one of the top singles players in tennis, and then she moved on to team with Martina Navratilova. She enjoyed success as a television commentator and now cherishes her life as a wife and mother. Through it all, she coped with the death of a husband and the disappointments that come with testing yourself at the highest levels of a career. As she told me, life has its ups and downs, and you'd better be able to deal with the bad times and get everything back together, because no one is going to be able to do it for you.

As an aside, when I was leaving her house, her oldest son hit a golf ball off the cement, right into a hedge. The glow on her face showed that she was one proud mom.

ANNIKA SORENSTAM

B Y ANY STANDARD, Sweden's Annika Sorenstam is one
of the greatest players in LPGA history. A member of
the World Golf Hall of Fame, she came into the 2007 season with sixty-nine victories, including ten wins in major
championships. The 1994 Rolex Rookie of the Year, she is
an eight-time LPGA Player of the Year and the winner of
six Vare Trophies for low scoring average. She has also rep-
resented Europe on seven Solheim Cup teams. In 2008 she
announced that, for all intents and purposes, she was retiring from competitive golf.

One of my first memories of Annika is of a 1994 pro-am
in Sacramento. I remember being impressed by how metic-
ulous she was at breakfast. She had fruit, juice, an egg, and
cereal. I thought that anyone who prepared that properly
for breakfast—and took such good care of herself—would
certainly be prepared on the golf course. From that obser-
vation, I was pretty sure that she would be very successful

because I could see that she was a perfectionist, and was a little bit selfish, which you need to be if you hope to be successful as a professional golfer.

We sat down to talk in the press room at Mission Hills Country Club during the 2007 Kraft Nabisco Championship, a major she and I both have won three times. Although I hadn't spent much time with her over the years, we have always had a special connection, because we were both dedicated to our careers and I thought she appreciated my freewheeling style. She is a good listener and, as I expected, her answers were very precise and carefully thought out. What I didn't expect was her openness and her sense of humor. I began our conversation by telling her my recollection of seeing her at breakfast in Sacramento.

*   *   *

I've always been very organized. Going back to my school days, my books would be in my backpack before I had to leave for school and they would be stacked neatly in my locker at school. My lockers on tour are the same way. Very organized. My thinking is the same way, whether it's about golf or my outside activities. I take everything step-by-step, like climbing a ladder. I need to know where I'm going. Before I do anything, I want to have as much information as possible, because information is the most powerful tool you can have. You can't just absorb it like a sponge. You have to know what to take and what to ignore, but the big thing is you can't be afraid to listen and grow.

I think it's very important to always be learning and seeking knowledge. If you don't, I think something is wrong. I see every day as a chance to learn something new. The past is good for experience, but you can't live in the past, except to build on your victories to build your confidence. I try every day to live in the present and prepare for the future.

Annika has a reputation of being one of the hardest workers on our tour. I asked if, like her preparation, that has always been the case.

Yes, very much so. Our family was comfortable but certainly not wealthy. I always worked in summers so I could afford the clubs I wanted. I think that's better than just having them handed to you. If you work for something, you know its value. That's why I work so hard on the golf course. It helps me appreciate the results of that hard work even more.

I wondered if her parents had pushed her and her sister [her younger sister, Charlotta, is also an LPGA member] into sports.

Not at all. They exposed us to sports and made it possible for us to have lessons, but it was always up to us if we wanted to pursue a sport. It was like I was in a frame they kept at arm's length. They would take me to tennis tournaments or soccer matches and be very supportive, but if I lost, they were very understanding. They just wanted me to have fun. They weren't like Little League parents who scream and yell at their kids.

In 2003, Annika became the first woman to play in the PGA Tour event since Babe Zaharias in 1945. There was some criticism of both Annika and the Bank of America Colonial, but even though she shot rounds of 71 and 75 and missed the cut, she was widely praised for how she played and handled the intense media pressure.

I played Colonial because I wanted to challenge myself. I just wanted to raise the bar to see if I could clear it. At first there were some people who were critical, but that's just human nature. There are always going to be people who question something new. I enjoyed myself. It was a lot of fun, and I think it helped me grow as a player and gave me an advantage on the LPGA Tour. I went out and had one of my best years. It's all part of growing. We're all presented with different paths to take, and Colonial was just one path that I decided to take.

One painful path Annika took was divorcing her husband after seven years of marriage. We spoke about how difficult it was and what she has learned from the experience.

It was hard because you don't have much of a chance to sit down and cry or think logically. I worked so hard to make it work. In some ways, it's like a round of golf. You work hard and give it your best. In the end, that's all you can do. I matured through the process, and that's important. Your life changes, and you have to be willing to accept the change. I never make any excuses. I don't understand people who make excuses for everything. You're in charge of the decisions you make, whether in your life or on the golf course. You can't blame anyone else. They're your decisions.

Knowing that she'd gone through a divorce, I thought it was interesting that when I asked her to name three people she'd like to have met, one was Diana, Princess of Wales. The other two were equally interesting choices. I found myself agreeing with her reasons for picking these people.

I think Diana had a very tough life. She married someone she loved and then was thrown into something she could never have expected, all under this incredible public scrutiny. Through it all she was very classy, which I think is amazing. I would have liked meeting her. Another person I really respect is Madonna. She's been around for a long time and has constantly reinvented herself to stay ahead of the pack. She's tough and she knows what she wants. She's also very good at controlling the Madonna brand. I admire that. The third person would be [former General Electric chairman and CEO] Jack Welch. He's one of the best leaders the country has. I'm fascinated by business and finance, and I've read all his books. I'm at the stage of my career where I have to think about life after competitive golf.

I want to start a family and would like probably two children. I want to experience that kind of loving and caring. Right now it's all about me. I also am focused on building the Annika brand and on my business future—golf schools, course design, my charities. This is very important for athletes, especially female athletes. Where do you go when your playing days are over? I want to be able to balance golf, my brand, and a family. I long for the day when I can get up, read the paper, watch TV, and just relax and not have to worry about shooting a 68. People have very high expectations of successful players, but sometimes you want to forget about their expectations and just take a break.

As our conversation wound down, I asked Annika if there was anything she might do differently if she had a chance to take a mulligan on her career.

When I came out on tour, Nancy Lopez was someone I really admired, but she was just so different from me in terms of personality. It was impossible for me to be like her. I knew I should try to be more open, but in Sweden you don't make a fuss about yourself—except Helen Alfredsson, who doesn't exactly have a Swedish personality. If I tried to be more like Nancy—very outgoing and expressive—it wouldn't have worked. But that didn't mean I didn't find winning very satisfying. It always gave me a little smile inside.

. . .

When I think of Annika Sorenstam, I'm struck by her willingness to grow and her clear vision for her future. Her curiosity, quest for knowledge, preparation, and work ethic—combined with her natural athleticism—have made her a great champion. I've always believed that one of the things that drive those who excel in any walk of life is the ability to reach a goal and then immediately set another one. They just love a challenge and aren't afraid to take it on. Annika not only dominated the LPGA but she won every tournament and honor worth winning. President John F. Kennedy used to say that when you see a patch of blue sky in the clouds—an opening—go for it. I have no doubt Annika will keep going for it as her playing days on the LPGA tour wind down.

KEN VENTURI

FOR TWO GENERATIONS of Americans, Ken Venturi is best known as a golf analyst for CBS Sports, a position he held from 1968 until his retirement in 2002—a stretch that made him the longest-serving television analyst in any sport. But his sixty years in golf go far beyond his television career. He was a brilliant player who enjoyed success as an amateur and as a young professional, then went into a slump from which few expected him to recover. Yet he did recover, coming back to win the 1964 U.S. Open in the cauldron of heat and pressure that made his victory among the most dramatic and poignant in the history of the championship. Though his playing career was ultimately cut short by injuries, the man who had learned to play from Byron Nelson and Ben Hogan went on to become a highly respected commentator and teacher. His countless acts of charity and kindness are largely unreported, but he has been an inspiration to golfers and non-golfers alike for his courage and perseverance.

I was just a kid taking up the game when Ken won his Open, and I remember following it in the newspapers. I first saw him on television when he was a part of the old *CBS Golf Classic*—a weekly program I tried never to miss. We met many times since then as our lives overlapped, but until I sat down with Ken and his wife, Kathleen, at their home in Rancho Mirage, California, there was much I didn't know about him and his life. I came away with an increased respect and admiration for a remarkable man. We began by talking about his boyhood in San Francisco, and I was surprised to learn that his first love was baseball.

.   .   .

I loved baseball, and when I was eighteen, Lefty O'Doul, who was the Yankees' scout in San Francisco, offered me a contract to play centerfield. Years earlier, when I was in grammar school, I was diagnosed as having an incurable stammer. I stuttered so badly that I could barely get a sentence out. My mother was told I would never be able to speak. She asked me what I was going to do. I had been caddying and loved golf, so I told her I was going to "take up the loneliest sport I know." I could play and practice by myself. I would pretend I was an announcer. "Here's Ken Venturi, with a putt to win the U.S. Open." It's funny that it was always the Open. That's how I taught myself to talk. I was fine when I was on the baseball field, but on the bus trips the kids would tease me unmercifully. Stammering is the only handicap people still make fun of, and it is brutal for kids. I always joke that I pursued golf over baseball because country clubs were nicer than dugouts, but the truth is I didn't want to take any more of the teasing.

I asked Ken if he was a natural when it came to golf.

My father gave me two rules I had to follow: the first was to count every single stroke—whiffs and everything—and the other was to play fast. My first round of golf was at Harding Park [a municipal course in San Francisco]. I shot a 172 and went home and told my father I had counted every stroke and we never held anyone up. That was good enough for him. I always had a really good short game, and ironically part of that was due to my stammering. We know now that it can be caused by taking a natural lefty and making him switch to being a righty. It creates an imbalance in a part of the brain that affects speech. The plus side for me is that I became ambidextrous, which helped my short game.

We talked about the role Byron Nelson played in developing his game.

Byron was good friends with Eddie Lowery, who owned the biggest car dealership in San Francisco and was a supporter of mine. They had come to watch me play in the 1952 U.S. Amateur in Seattle, where I lost in the first round. The next day Nelson invited me to play a round with him at San Francisco Golf Club. I shot a 66, which I thought was pretty good. When we finished, I kept expecting him to tell me how well I played. He didn't. Finally, with all the cockiness of a twenty-one-year-old, I asked him what he thought. I was stunned when he told me that there were seven or eight things I needed to work on and we'd start the next morning. A beautiful friendship was born that day. Byron taught me about a lot more than golf.

Ken first came to national attention at the 1956 Masters, which he almost won as an amateur. He wound up finishing second. It was a finish that changed his life forever.

I had a 4-stroke lead going into the final round. In those days, the leader was always paired with Byron, but since he was my mentor, Bob Jones and Cliff Roberts didn't think that would be appropriate. They asked me who I'd like to play with. I figured that since I had been taught by Byron and played so many rounds with Ben Hogan, Sam Snead was the logical choice. If I was going to walk up eighteen as the champion, I wanted it to be beside another champion. Over the years, people have said Sam was tough on me in the final round. That's not true. Sam tried to talk with me, but he could see how nervous I was, so he left me alone. And I had good reason to be nervous. The conditions were horrible. It was windy and cold, and I never felt comfortable on the greens. Still, I hit fifteen greens in regulation and had an 8-stroke lead at the turn. But then everything fell apart on the back nine. I wound up 3-putting six times for the round. While I was on my way to an 80, Jackie Burke shot a 71, the only round under par for the day, and beat me by a stroke. Bob Jones told me that if I had won the tournament, I would have been the next chairman of Augusta National. The plan was for me to become a vice president at Ford Motors. I would have made millions. I would never have turned pro and never have won the Open.

Years later, I was honored at a dinner for the Collegiate Golf Hall of Fame at the Waldorf-Astoria in New York. Jack Whitaker introduced me. He said something that has always stuck with me: "Fate has a way of bending the twig and fashioning a man to his best instincts." I know that's true in my life.

Ken told me that it was at the 1954 Masters that he became friends with Ben Hogan.

On the first hole, he told me that if I had a short putt, just tap it in and don't wait for him to putt out because once he did, the galleries would take off running. He told me to call him Ben. I felt like a million bucks. Here I was playing in the Masters with my new friend, Ben. Everything went along fine until the par-3 fourth hole. I hit first and put a 3-iron to four feet. Ben had been looking in my bag and hit a 3-iron, too. He put it in the front bunker. As we walked off the tee, he said, "It serves me right for watching an amateur. You've got a bag full of 1-irons." I thought, "This is great. I make a friend on the first hole and lose him on the fourth." I asked him if I should go back to calling him Mr. Hogan. He said no, but to give him my address after the round and he'd send me a set of clubs, which he did.

I loved Ben. I just liked the way he looked and carried himself. People ask what his secret was. It had nothing to do with his swing. He just out-thought and outworked everyone. I was honored that when Ben died, his wife, Valerie, called and told me I was his first choice to serve as one of the honorary pallbearers.

After turning pro in 1957, Ken quickly became one of the Tour's most successful players, winning ten tournaments from 1957 through 1960. But a 1962 car accident injured his back, and by 1963 his swing and his marriage were deteriorating. He went into a spiral of despair. The turning point came on a barstool back home in San Francisco.

I remember it like it was yesterday. It was a cold, dreary afternoon in September 1963. I was sitting alone at the Tropics Bar on Geary Street. The bartender was Dave Marcelli, a former football star at the University of San Francisco, and a friend I admired. I was keeping company with my new best friend, Jack Daniel's. I asked Dave for a drink and instead got a lecture that saved my life. Dave asked me what I was doing to myself. He said I had all the talent in the world and everyone was pulling for me but I was pissing my life away. Dave wasn't telling me anything I didn't know, but it sank in. Finally, I asked him for a double. I sat there nursing that drink for a couple of hours. Finally I stood up, leaned over the bar, and dropped the glass in the trash can. I promised Dave then and there that I would never take another drink until I won again—and I didn't until ten months later, when I won the Open and celebrated with a glass of wine. And I haven't had a drop of Jack Daniel's since that day at the bar.

That day I thought a lot about what my father had always told me: "Quitting is the only thing in life that doesn't take any talent. Anyone can do it," and I wasn't going to be a quitter.

The story of Ken's climb back to the top and his win in the Open is one of the most dramatic in any sport. As he told me, his progress was slow but his determination never wavered. There were ups and downs, but a crucial, make-or-break moment came at Westchester Country Club outside New York. Ken had gotten in on the last sponsor's exemption. In contention on the last day, he came to the difficult par-3 sixteenth and faced a difficult choice—one of the toughest of his playing career.

The safe play was to hit a 4-iron and take the trouble out of play, pitch up, hope for a 3 and settle for a 4. At least I'd take a big number out of the picture. But I knew this was *the* moment. I told myself that if I backed off now, I'd be backing off for the rest of my life. I hit a perfect 3-iron. I missed the putt for birdie, but I had proven something to myself. The third-place money gave me a cushion going into the Open.

The 1964 Open was the last year the USGA played thirty-six holes on Saturday. The heat reached 105 degrees and the humidity was unbearable. Ken went out in 30 in the morning round, but by the fourteenth hole, the pressure and the conditions began to take their toll. On the fourteenth hole, he began to tremble. By the seventeenth hole, he was hallucinating. He lined up a two-footer and saw three holes. He putted toward the middle hole and missed. He also bogeyed the last hole but still shot a 66.

As Ken tried to recuperate in the clubhouse between rounds, Dr. John Knowles told him, "If you go back out there, you could very easily die."

"Doc," Ken said, "I'm already dying. I've got no place else to go."

He went out in 35 and took the lead. By the seventeenth hole, he was again on the verge of collapse.

As I walked off the tee I told Joe Dey [the director of the USGA] that he could put two strokes on me for slow play, but I couldn't walk any faster. He told me, "Ken, it's all downhill to the eighteenth green. Now how about holding your chin up, so when you come in as a champion, you'll look like one."

In one of the most dramatic moments in golf history, Ken Venturi putted out on the last hole, dropped his putter, raised his arms toward heaven, and said, "My God, I've won the Open."

Ken went on to win two more tournaments that year, but he had begun experiencing numbness in his fingers. It was diagnosed as carpal tunnel syndrome, and doctors at the Mayo Clinic warned him that he might never play golf again or, worse, might have some of his fingers amputated.

I went home to San Francisco to get my affairs in order. My father drove me to the airport. I was scared to death. We got out of the car and hugged. He looked me right in the eyes and said, "Son, it doesn't matter if you never play golf again. You were the best I ever saw." That was the first time he had ever praised me. Suddenly, nothing else mattered. When I got to the hospital, the doctor was amazed by my attitude. I told him, "Doc, my father told me I was good. That's all that matters. I'm ready for whatever happens."

Curiously, Ken's last PGA Tour victory came in the 1966 Lucky International at Harding Park, the course where he played his first round of golf. He tried to play the Tour for the next two years, but the effects of the carpal tunnel syndrome prevented him from ever regaining his top form. When CBS offered him the commentator's job, he accepted—in part so that he could serve as an example for kids who stuttered. As our time together ended, my last question was how golf has changed his life.

When I look back, it made me into who or what I am. Not as a player, but as a person. I learned that I don't have to be better than everyone else. I just have to be better than I thought I could be.

. . .

When you look at Ken Venturi's life, you see the importance of having the courage to persevere. He could easily have fallen into the trap of self-pity and simply given up. In fact, as I learned, he almost did. But what always pulled him back from the edge was the enormous pride that it takes to become a great champion. Ken's life has many important lessons to teach us all, but for my money, the lesson of courage lost and courage found is by far the most profound.

Something else struck me during my visit with Ken. When he talked about how important his father's approval was to him, I was reminded of how important my parents' approval was to me. That kind of unconditional love is huge and a good lesson for children and parents alike. I thought of the story that Greg Louganis, the Olympic Gold Medal–winning diver, tells about the dive he faced to win the gold. He needed a perfect 10. As he prepared to dive, he thought, "No matter what happens, my mother will still love me."

His dive was perfect. So was his mother's love.

ROBERT WAGNER

R OBERT WAGNER—or R.J., as he's known to his friends—
is a legend of film and television.

Born in Detroit, he moved to Los Angeles at an early
age. One of his earliest jobs was working as a caddie, and
among the people he caddied for was Clark Gable, which
allowed him to see what Hollywood stars are like in real
life.

He got his start in films when he made a brief but memorable appearance in *With a Song in My Heart.* Spencer Tracy
saw him in *Beneath the 12-Mile Reef* and requested Wagner for the role of his son in *Broken Lance.* Tracy was so
impressed with Wagner that he cast him as his brother in
The Mountain. He has made more than one hundred films,
and some of my favorites are the Austin Powers comedies,
in which he plays the eyepatch-wearing Number Two, an
enemy of Mike Myers's title character. Wagner is hilarious
in these—just as he is offscreen. In fact, he's one of the fun-

niest people I know. I'll never forget the time he came up to me at Bel-Air and said, "Amy, you're so beautiful. Do you mind if I come over there and grope you?" It broke me up and all the people who were around. The other film I really like is *Banning*, which he made in 1967, where he plays a golf professional in Los Angeles. When you see him in that movie, you can see just how good a golfer he really is.

While he has had a successful film career, he's probably best known to most people for his roles in three hugely successful television series: *It Takes a Thief*, with Fred Astaire; *Switch*, with Eddie Albert and Sharon Gless; and *Hart to Hart*, with Stefanie Powers.

Following the tragic drowning death of his wife, Natalie Wood, in 1981, Wagner married actress Jill St. John in 1991. They live in a ranch house in Brentwood, which is where I visited with them. At one point during my visit, he showed me around the house, which is like a museum of show business history. There are photos of him with legends like Cary Grant and, of course, Natalie Wood, as well as movie memorabilia, a painting of him as a young man, and some photos of his winning horses.

· · ·

I know you started playing at a young age. How did that shape your personality and character?

When I was a kid, my family had a membership at Detroit Golf Club, where Tommy Armour was the professional. My father loved the game, and I started playing when I was six. When we moved to Los Angeles, we joined Bel-Air. It was during World War II, and they got local kids to caddie. There were so many people from the industry at Bel-Air that it probably helped spark my interest in acting.

Golf had a lot to do with shaping who I am today. The game teaches you patience and humility; and being around older golfers, a young person learns etiquette and manners. Plus, you learn to play by the rules, which is a good lesson in the real world. I think golf teaches young people a lot of valuable lessons. I know it taught me a great deal.

Tell me about your role in Banning. *I think that's one of the few believable movies about golf.*

The reason most golf movies don't work is that the studios cast actors who don't have a clue about the game, and they are complicated movies to make. I hit every one of my own shots. There was no double. We shot it at Riviera and Lakeside.

In the movie, your character isn't afraid to play for a little of his own money. I know you're the same way.

I love gambling. I bet on everything—football, baseball, cards. I really like baseball because it's so unpredictable. The worst team can beat the best team on any given day. I love to go to Vegas and play at the craps tables. I just love the action. I used to gamble a lot more when I was single, but I don't bet as much now.

You're obviously still a good player, but you once told me that you used to walk away from the game for years at a time. Why was that?

When I was young, I'd play or hit balls, play cards, chase women, and drink booze. Life was pretty good. Then my marriage to Natalie [Wood] broke up and I kind of woke up. I moved to Europe and put the clubs away. I came back to L.A. at one point and saw people standing in the same spots saying the same things. It was kind of an epiphany. I realized I had to start reading some books and turning my life in a different direction. I did start playing again, but when my daughter, Katie, was born I stopped. Even when I wasn't playing, golf was in my soul.

Since so much of your life has involved both acting and golf, I was wondering if they complemented each other.

When I look back, I think I took up acting because I needed a lot of attention. In the beginning, I apprenticed. I had a lot of bit parts, but that's how I learned and developed my craft. The more I acted, the more I began to realize how miraculous the process is when it all comes together.

It's like when I go to a play and see a great performance. In acting, you have your script and your fellow actors. You're reacting, to an extent. It's more like tennis, where you hit it, someone hits it back, and you react. In golf, you're on your own. It's a sport where you have to compensate all the time. In acting, you read the script and you know what's going to happen. The trick is making people think it's the first time you've done it and that you're not really acting. If people are aware you're acting, then it's bad acting. You have to be in the moment when you're acting. Everyone has their own timing and rhythm.

What have you learned from both acting and golf over the years?

In life, you go through a lot of stages. It's human nature to get angry and down, just like you do on the golf course. There are times you think you'll never hit another good shot and then it just appears. Also, in the last twenty-five years, my expectations in life haven't been as high, so life is more fun. I know that's true in my golf. My expectations aren't nearly as high anymore.

Who are some of the memorable people you've played with?

I loved playing with Fred Astaire at Bel-Air. As you can imagine, he had wonderful rhythm. So did Bing Crosby. Bing could really play. Clint Eastwood is great to play with because he just loves the game so much. I was playing with him when I made a hole in one at Cypress Point. I played with Ben Hogan and Sam Snead. I actually beat Sam, and he never forgot it, either. I played with Gary Player. What a terrific guy. He's so enthusiastic and optimistic. I actually played with Arnold Palmer and Jack Nicklaus at the same time. Jack knew he could be intimidating. When we were playing he said to me, "Think about this: you have a chance to win a tournament and you're about to hit a shot and I'm standing here watching you." He was right. It was intimidating.

Has anyone ever made you feel uncomfortable on the course?

I was playing in the Crosby Pro-Am one year with Billy Casper. I had to keep stopping because people wanted autographs. He said, "You know, there is a golf tournament going on." I apologized, but I mean, come on, it's the Crosby.

Is it true that you once planned to build a golf course?

I used to raise cutting horses on a ranch up near the Reagan Library. I had 184 acres. It's where Seabiscuit is buried. I talked to Tom Fazio about designing the course. Tom's a friend, and he said he'd do it for free on one condition: that I not invest any of my own money in the project. He said that the planning and zoning process would be a nightmare and it would be almost impossible to get it built. I realized he was right. It's too bad. It would have been a wonderful location for a course.

At this point in your life, do you feel comfortable in your own skin?

Pretty much. Life is good, and I love doing the Austin Powers movies. That part was made for me.

. . .

What struck me after I spoke with R.J. was how his incredibly dry, witty sense of humor has helped him get through a lot, in both his personal and his professional lives, and it reminded me of the importance of finding humor in all things, even in a game like golf.

KARRIE WEBB

I N 2005, AUSTRALIA'S KARRIE WEBB, age thirty, became
the youngest member of the LPGA to be inducted
into the World Golf Hall of Fame—and it was an honor
she richly deserved. Through the end of the 2007 season,
she had thirty-five career victories, including six majors.
In 2001, she became the youngest player to complete the
LPGA's Career Grand Slam. In addition, she has won three
Vare Trophies for the lowest scoring average in a season,
as well as two Rolex Player of the Year Awards. Karrie's
latest victory came in the 2006 Kraft Nabisco Championship, when she holed a pitching wedge for an eagle on
the seventy-second hole and then beat Lorena Ochoa on
the first playoff hole. She went on to win five other tournaments that year, ending a slump that saw her win just
one tournament in both the 2003 and 2004 seasons and
go without a win in 2005. I asked Karrie if anger had had
anything to do with her comeback in 2006.

. . .

I don't think it comes from anger. Technically, it was a result of all the hard work I put in during the off-season. Fortunately, golf has been good enough to me that I don't have to put up with playing badly. I'm not just out here to help make up the field. I know I'm better than that. I recognized that I had to make some changes to get back to where I was, and I gave myself a timetable to do that. I mean, I was having years that most players would love to have, but I didn't want that. I knew I was better than the way I was playing.

Were you just getting in your own way?

Yes, I think so. I was just trying too hard.

Are you a spiritual person when it comes to golf?

I'm not sure what you mean. I believe everything is predestined. I'll tell you an interesting thing about my win in last year's Nabisco. I had dreams that I had a seven-foot, left-to-right-breaking putt on the last hole to win that tournament. I could see myself making that putt on the eighteenth hole, with all the people in the stands. I practiced that putt all the time and would tell myself, "This is to win the Nabisco." As it turned out, I didn't have to putt on the eighteenth hole because I holed my approach, but I did make that identical putt to beat Lorena in the playoff. I didn't think about it at the time, but shortly after I won, it occurred to me. I don't know if that's spiritual, but it's pretty interesting.

Did having such a great 2006 season after three seasons that, by your standards, weren't very good teach you anything?

I don't think I ever took my success for granted, but it did help me understand that there is such a fine line between good and bad or success and failure.

Tell me a little bit about how you got started playing golf.

When I was very young, probably about four, I was given a set of little plastic clubs, and then for my eighth birthday my parents gave me a cut-down set of clubs. I played all the sports as a kid. I even studied tap-dancing, but nothing ever took me like golf.

Do you think you've always been a competitive person?

Yes, in whatever I did. I'm the oldest child, and I think the oldest in particular always want to please their parents.

Did you play to please your parents or grandparents? I know you were close to your grandfather.

Certainly, I hoped they'd be proud of me, but honestly, I think motivation comes from within. I love the game of golf and I knew if I worked hard I'd give myself chances to win. My parents have been very supportive, but if I decided I didn't want to play, they'd be supportive of me for making that decision. I know I've given them a lot of joy, and I know they sometimes scratch their heads wondering how they ever produced someone who could play the way I do. Honestly, though, I never felt any pressure to play well for them.

Obviously you've had a lot of success, but golf also provides its share of disappointments. Is there one that stands out in your mind?

Probably the 1997 Australian Masters. It was a first-year LPGA event and I had only been a pro for two years, but the Australian media was focused on when I was going to win and if I was going to win this tournament. I came to the final three holes with a 3-stroke lead and 3-putted seventeen and eighteen to lose by a stroke. I won it the next year, but that was a tough loss because I didn't get the job done.

I think amateurs don't understand the psychology of playing really well, of posting a good score. When you're 3- or 4-under after six holes, do you think about going as low as you possibly can?

I think it's just a matter of where you are mentally at the time. Sometimes you're just oblivious to everything, especially the score. Other days you're very conscious of everything. Obviously, it's easier when you're just in a zone and not thinking. You're just kind of in the moment.

Does it scare you when you're playing so well?

Sometimes, but that's what we play for. I remember the one time I had a chance to shoot a 59. I tried not to get too excited but I wound up parring the last three holes.

Does anything scare you?

You mean like death? No, that's going to happen to everyone. I used to think that if you couldn't walk you'd be better off dead, but seeing the example set by Christopher Reeve [she helped to found and organize the annual Karrie Webb Celebrity Pro-Am to benefit the Christopher Reeve Paralysis Foundation] and my coach, Kevin Haller, who is a quadriplegic, I definitely don't believe that any longer. Kevin's life has been altered from what he thought it would be, but he has a healthy family and grandkids. If he'd died, he wouldn't have experienced any of that. Seeing that changed my thinking about life entirely.

· · ·

After speaking with Karrie Webb, I was reminded of how much of our success—and our ability to recover from disappointment—comes from within us. Karrie obviously

AMY ALCOTT

wanted to please her parents and bring them joy with her success, but it is her inner will that helped her become a champion—which is difficult enough—and also to regain her place at the top of the game, which is often even more of a challenge. In the end, golf is like life in this way: you are given chances to reinvent yourself if you have the vision and courage to do so. Karrie certainly did.

SANDY WEILL

O NE OF THE most fascinating people I've met in all these years is Sandy Weill, who became the chief executive officer and chairman of Citigroup, Inc., and today serves as the corporation's chairman emeritus. He is a giant—even a legend—in the global financial markets and has earned well-deserved praise for his work as a philanthropist in the areas of education, health care, and the arts. All in all, remarkable accomplishments for a man who grew up in Brooklyn as the son of immigrant parents from Eastern Europe.

I met Sandy in the early 1980s, when he was with American Express. I was paired with Sandy in an outing held by his friend Lewis Rudin, one of the most influential people in New York City's real estate market, a passionate golfer, and a peach of a guy. We played at Deepdale and hit it off right away. We shared a lot of jokes and a lot of laughs, and our personalities just clicked. It probably helped that he looks a lot like my father, Eugene. I was also relieved when I noticed that his shoes were a little on the scruffy side. My mother was always reminding me that my shoes should be shined, but I figured that if a scuff mark or two was good enough for Sandy, it was good enough for me.

I felt I had made a friend, so I would call him once or twice a year just to stay in touch. The first thing he'd always ask was if I had any good jokes for him—and I made sure I always did. Sandy was very generous with advice, and I always felt that he mentored me without even knowing it . . . or maybe he did know.

Though Sandy has been very successful, he's also had his share of setbacks, but I think that's probably inevitable when you aim high. I can relate to that because I've had my share of slumps, dips, and disappointments—just enough to help me truly appreciate my successes.

I don't really believe in coincidences, and I think I was destined to meet Sandy, not only because he resembled my dad but because he was a mentor for me from a distance, as I read about him and watched how he conducted his life.

Sandy will be the first to admit that he's not a great golfer, but he enjoys the game, and when you play with him you really appreciate his people skills, which, in the end, are probably a big reason for his success. When I think of Sandy Weill, I think of a quotation from Will Rogers that's posted in Will Rogers State Park near my home in Los Angeles: "It's great to be great, but it's greater to be human."

We met in early May in Sandy's office on the forty-sixth floor of the GM Building on Fifth Avenue and Fifty-ninth Street in Manhattan. The city was just starting to take on its spring colors, and the view of Central Park was stunning. It was a bright, clear day, and looking north from the park you could see Yankee Stadium in the distance. To the west was the Hudson River and, beyond that, New Jersey.

As we walked from the large reception area to Sandy's office, I saw that the walls were lined with photographs of him with presidents and political and civic leaders from around the world, and letters and proclamations, all of which serve as testimony to a life well and significantly lived.

In the course of our hour together, I was struck by how quickly his mind worked. It was almost as though he could anticipate my questions, and in many cases he answered before I finished asking them. I was also struck by the sense of quiet power he exuded. He was charming and very matter-of-fact . . . and yes, he did ask if I had any jokes for him.

· · ·

I played tennis as a kid and didn't really take up golf until I was in my thirties, which is pretty late to learn a sport as demanding as golf. When you take up the game that late in life, the only way you can become really good is to practice a lot, and my career didn't give me enough spare time for that. But I do enjoy the game and have met a lot of interesting people through it.

I played in the old Crosby tournament in the last two years before it became the AT&T Pebble Beach National Pro-Am. The first time I played in the Crosby I was paired with Hal Sutton, whom I've become very good friends with. We were paired with former president Gerald Ford and Jack Nicklaus, and I remember standing on the first tee at Cypress Point thinking, "Here we are, three blond guys and me." I didn't exactly get off to an encouraging start. My ball was in my pocket on the first hole and on the second hole, too. But on the par-3 third hole I was twelve feet from the hole. Jack was eight feet from the hole, and Hal was off the green. Hal chipped in for a 2. I was lining up my putt when Jack looked at me and said, "Can you beat a 2?"—meaning he wanted me to pick up so he could putt. It made me mad and I became very competitive. Hal and I played very well, and we were a stroke off the lead going into Sunday's final round. We didn't do so well and I think we finished twelfth, but it was fun while it lasted.

The other thing I remember about playing with President Ford was that one of his shots hit a woman on the top of her head. He was very concerned and embarrassed, but the woman was fine. I told him I was as concerned as he was because Travelers [where Sandy was president] carried his insurance, putting him under Sandy's umbrella, so to speak.

Another memory I have from Pebble Beach was the year I was in the group behind Congressman Dan Rostenkowski, then one of the most powerful Democrats in the country. We saw someone talk to him and he began walking back to the clubhouse in a hurry. He had just been told that the space shuttle *Challenger* had exploded. Most times the golf course is a good place to get away from the real world, but not always.

I asked Sandy if he had a favorite course, and I wasn't surprised when he said it was Augusta National Golf Club.

I love all the tradition and history that is so much a part of Augusta. It really hits you when you turn down Magnolia Lane for the first time. And even though you're familiar with the course, having watched the Masters so often, nothing prepares you for the beauty of the place, the changes in elevation and the contours. I don't think there's another course quite like it. Another thing I love is that there's a very relaxed atmosphere at Augusta. It's a place you can put your feet up and relax. One year I was staying in one of the cabins, which are very tasteful and low-key. I shared a bedroom with Jim Robinson, the chairman of American Express, but it was pretty small and the beds were fairly close together.

He woke me with his snoring. I tried to get him to roll over, which usually works when my wife is breathing loudly.

"Turn, turn, turn," I said.

The next morning he asked me if I realized I talked in my sleep.

"You were practicing your swing," he said. "You kept saying 'Turn, turn, turn.'"

I was interested in learning how golf related to Sandy's approach to business and life.

I think that learning how to concentrate is very important in both life and business, and that is something you can learn through golf because you have so much time between shots. If you can't concentrate, you're not going to play very well. Golf is a great way to bond with people, and I think you can learn how a person chooses to live their life by how they approach golf. In my case, I think it's okay to make a mistake as long as you learn from it. If you're afraid to take a chance, you'll lay up all the time. Life is a risk-reward proposition, and you have to be able to carefully evaluate risk. You have to honestly ask yourself if you're happier drifting through life and settling for a place in the middle of the pack. I'm not, and fortunately it's worked out pretty well. In the end, though, I've come to realize that golf is like life because they're both just games. You can't take yourself too seriously. You've got to be able to relax and let it go.

As Sandy and I spoke, my eyes drifted to one photo in particular on his wall. It appeared to have been taken in the 1940s and showed a modest house in a city neighborhood. The photo was located directly across from Sandy's desk.

That's the three-family house I grew up in. It was in Bensonhurst, Brooklyn, and we lived on the second floor. I keep it to remind me of my roots and help me appreciate what I have today.

. . .

That appreciation has led Sandy to focus his attention on philanthropic activities. For many years he was a trustee at his alma mater, Cornell University, and in 1998 he and his wife of more than fifty years, Joan, endowed the university's medical school, which is now known as the Joan and Sanford I. Weill Medical College and Graduate School of Medical Science. He is the chairman of the Carnegie Hall board of directors. He created the National Academy Foundation, whose mission is to change and reform education. Among his other successes are the establishment of a medical school in Qatar and a hospital and medical school in Tanzania. Beyond the humanitarian value of these efforts, he stresses that he sees activities like these as a means of bridging cultural differences between people and nations. He quite candidly told me that he and his wife plan to give away most of their fortune in their philanthropic efforts.

To me, this willingness to give back to society is something we can all take away from the life of Sandy Weill. He loves life and could easily spend the rest of his days enjoying anything money can buy. Instead, because he understands the ethos of giving, he wants to leave a mark as profound in the lives of others as he made in corporate America. I have no doubt that he will.

JERRY WEINTRAUB

OVER THE YEARS I've met a lot of interesting people, and Jerry Weintraub is one of the most unforgettable. He's a larger-than-life figure who seems like he could have been a character in one of the many movies he's produced over the years.

Jerry grew up in New York, the son of a gem salesman. He learned the craft of salesmanship from his father, and has elevated it to an art form. In the course of our long and rambling conversation, he insisted that he is the "best salesman in the world," and I have no reason to doubt him. He is also an extraordinary deal maker, schmoozer, and people person.

He began his career as a talent agent for MCA in the 1950s and went on to represent clients as diverse as talk-show host Jack Paar and singer Jane Morgan. He and two partners formed Management III in 1965, beginning with just three clients. He later became a major concert promoter, and after he founded Concerts West, he handled Elvis Presley, Frank Sinatra, Bob Dylan, Led Zeppelin, the Beach Boys, and others.

In the 1970s, he branched out into movie production, beginning with Robert Altman's *Nashville* in 1975; that was followed by *Oh, God!,* starring George Burns; *9/30/55; Cruising;* and *All Night Long.* In 1982, he produced *Diner,* which introduced acting talents Kevin Bacon, Paul Reiser, Mickey Rourke, Tim Daly, Ellen Barkin, and Steve Guttenberg. He has produced more than one hundred television specials, perhaps most notably *Sinatra: The Main Event.* He has also appeared in numerous films, including *The Firm, National Lampoon's Vegas Vacation,* and *Ocean's Eleven,* which he produced, along with all the sequels.

In March 1991, President George H. W. Bush appointed Jerry to the board of the John F. Kennedy Center for the Performing Arts, and he is actively involved in a great deal of charity and philanthropic work.

We met at his home, which overlooks Palm Springs, and began our conversation by talking about growing up in New York.

.   .   .

I played a lot of sports, but not golf. I didn't see a course until I was twenty. I did a lot of different jobs, but I always seemed to be working. I remember setting pins in a bowling alley, but I really got my start in business when I was around twelve or thirteen. I used to deliver groceries. You'd get tips, and back then fifteen cents was a big tip. There was a Chinese laundry in the neighborhood, and I figured I could make more money if I delivered people's laundry with their groceries. Business was so good, I had to hire some of my friends from school. I split their tips with them fifty-fifty. I had a lot of fun and made about ten dollars a week.

Did that give you confidence?

I still don't have a lot of confidence. It just seems like I re-invented myself every ten years or so. The important thing is that I use everything I learned in my different businesses to move to the next plateau.

Is that the secret to your success?

Part of it. I think I have sort of a disarming charm. I'm a character, I admit it. Creative people, athletes, successful people like to be around me. And I'm not afraid of anything. I'm the best salesman in the world, and if I believe in something I can sell it. If I hear "no," it means "yes" to me. And I've always had these great, crazy ideas. When I was a kid I'd tell people my ideas and they'd say, "What are you, nuts?" That's what they said when I started producing rock concerts, but it was a huge success and it led me to starting record companies and music publishing. That was another success. Like I said, everything I do builds on what I've done and what I've learned.

And you've become one of the most powerful people in the entertainment business. . . .

I don't have any power. I have a lot of friends. The bottom line is that the entertainment business is a people business. When I decided to produce *Ocean's Eleven,* people thought I was out of my mind. They said I'd never be able to assemble the team of talent I put together. I knew I could. Do you know why it worked? Because I made it a happy atmosphere for everyone. They [the actors] established great relationships with each other and they are all very supportive of me. They want to take care of Grandpa. It used to be Dad but I'll be seventy pretty soon, so it's Grandpa. The first President Bush is another great example of how friendship works.

How?

I consider him a great friend and one of the most honest, moral people I've ever met. He took a Jewish kid from Brooklyn and welcomed him into his world. I have a home in Kennebunkport [Maine] and I couldn't get into the local golf club. He got me in. I'll never forget that. I think he likes me because I can figure out people really quickly. I'll tell you a great George Bush story. When he was president he called and told me he was coming to Los Angeles for a short visit and wanted to play golf, do a little fishing, and have a few people over for dinner. As a courtesy, he invited President Reagan to join us, and he accepted, which was a surprise. We teed off at Sherwood around seven, and early in the round, one of President Reagan's shoes broke. I asked him what size he wore and he said he didn't know. He hadn't bought a pair of shoes in forty years. We called the pro shop and had them send us every pair of shoes between sizes ten and thirteen.

What are some of your other memorable golf experiences?

I didn't take up the game until I was twenty, but I had a hole in one the first time I played. I used to play at a course in New Jersey. The mob guys used the course as a place where they could arrange payoffs from the casinos in Las Vegas, because you can't wiretap a golf course. All these guys in suits would get in golf carts and drive down the first fairway. Once they got over the hill and they couldn't be seen, they'd split up thousands of dollars. There was a road that ran by the hole, and one day as they were splitting up the money, a truck drove by and backfired. Ten guys fell on the ground in panic. I love it.

What's the best tip you ever got?

I've had tips from everyone. It's always the last one that works, but most of the lessons I get only work when the pro is there. My big problem is I can't concentrate long enough. Anyway, one of the two best lessons I've had came from Jimmy Demaret. He was the pro at the Concord Hotel in the Catskills and I was a busboy, which was the greatest job in the world if you were sixteen years old and Jewish. There were lots of women around, and their husbands were gone during the week. He liked me and we used to play. He had a beautiful MacGregor driver and he used to let me hit it. One day I hit a terrible drive and threw his driver. It hit a tree and the shaft broke. He looked like I just killed his child. He looked at me and said, "Jerry, I hope you learned a lesson just now. Don't ever throw a club." The other lesson came from Raymond Floyd. I had a tough shot from behind a tree. I was getting ready to play the shot and he told me, "Jerry, there's no tree in front of you. Just hit it."

Have you learned things from other athletes that you've been able to use either in golf or in business?

How important confidence is. I went out for dinner with Chris Evert and Jimmy Connors at Wimbledon when they were dating. She was going to face Tracy Austin in the finals, and *Sports Illustrated* had just run a cover story on her [Austin]. I asked Chrissie if she was worried. "Jerry, she can't beat me. She'll be crying when she leaves the court." Tiger Woods is the same way. I've heard that from Wayne Gretsky, Dorothy Hamill, Lance Armstrong, Ali, and others.

They all say their subconscious takes over. When Dorothy [Hamill] came home after winning the 1976 Olympics, I did a deal for her with Bristol-Myers. I was happy to do it because I liked her. I asked her what it was like knowing that you had worked your entire life to have it all hang on a four-minute routine. Imagine the pressure, knowing you have four minutes to prove yourself and pay off sixteen years of hard work? She said the last thing she remembered was hearing the announcer introduce her and after that she said it was like she was sitting in the stands watching herself perform. In the end, though, you need to know what you need to do to succeed. With great athletes, they need to know what to do to win. In my case, it's what I need to do to put a great deal together.

What do you think of Tiger Woods?

I think he's the best player of all time and I don't think he's even scratched the surface of what he can accomplish. He's so dominant. He's the total package. He's a fantastic star and spokesman for the game. He does everything just right. When he bears down, he'll kill you. The problem is that he's so dominant that when he doesn't play, there are no ratings.

Why do you think that is?

As a producer, I understand it. In the 1960s, you had the "Big Three," who were Jack Nicklaus, Arnold Palmer, and

Gary Player, so the quality of competition was so strong. Today there's so much money that there are no real characters. John Daly makes millions because he's a character. It seems like the players start so young and they're programmed. There's so much scrutiny in sports that it takes the personality out of golf. It reminds me of when I started out in the entertainment business. There were characters like Jack Warner and Mike Todd. I used to study P. T. Barnum's career. Today, everything is driven by the balance sheet. It's still an art form and an entertainment business. You still need creative people, but it's a different world today.

Do you gamble?

In business? All the time, but I know the odds. In golf, if someone wants to play a one-hundred-thousand-dollar Nassau, I can afford it, but I'd rather give the money to charity. Playing for twenty or twenty-five dollars is fine with me. I'm out there for the camaraderie. I want to play with people I can laugh with, not people who take it too seriously. I'm a member at Sunningdale, just outside London. I love the atmosphere there. It's what golf is all about for me. You get there around ten in the morning and have breakfast. There are about twenty guys and you go in groups. Lord so-and-so plays with the local plumber. There are people's dogs wandering around the course. You finish around four or five, drink for a while, and then have dinner and then play cards.

If you get a phone call, the steward doesn't bother you until the third time the person calls. In Europe, people take their golf seriously, but they take the camaraderie more seriously. I love it. It's my idea of what golf should be.

. . .

Jerry Weintraub uses his experiences as building blocks. In his career, he has learned from both his successes and his failures, and he's used those lessons to move on. Too often, I think people overlook their experiences and fail to learn from them. It's like in tournament golf. First you need to learn to play, and then you need to learn to compete and put yourself on the line. Finally, you need to learn how to win, and that's a part of being in contention and dealing with the setbacks. The successful players are those who can learn from setbacks, and it makes the winning sweeter . . . just as in life.

TOM WERNER

✦

MOST PEOPLE might not know my neighbor and friend Tom Werner by name, but they are certainly familiar with his work. He and his partner, Marcy Carsey, have produced some of the most popular television shows in recent history, including *Laverne & Shirley, Mork & Mindy, The Cosby Show, Roseanne,* and *Grace Under Fire.*

Of course, if you're a member of the Red Sox Nation, you know him as a co-owner of the group that bought the Sox and have seen them win two World Series. Almost as important, they dedicated themselves to preserving and improving Fenway Park, one of the true landmarks in any sport. I went to Fenway with Tom a couple of years ago, and if you are any kind of baseball fan, going to Fenway is something you should do at least once in your life.

We began our conversation by talking about his love for baseball.

. . .

One of my friends growing up was Rory Shor, whose father, Toots, owned a legendary saloon in New York City. Toots Shor's was more than a restaurant or bar; it was a place where celebrities, sports figures, and politicians gathered. I used to love to go there. One night Mickey Mantle and Willie Mays were there, and they autographed a ball for me. A few days later, Rory and I were going to play baseball in Central Park and we didn't have a ball. Rory convinced me to use my autographed ball. Of course, we lost it in some brambles, and I never got a replacement. Baseball has been one of the great loves of my life.

Did you root for the Yankees?

We all make mistakes when we're young. Actually, I switched to the Mets when they came along in the early 1960s.

What do you like about the game?

Baseball is very poetic. There are a lot of metaphors that apply to your life. The idea of running the bases only to return home is very powerful, don't you think? I also like it because it's a sport where teammates are very important. In basketball, one great player can carry a team. Just look at Michael Jordan. In baseball, everyone has to do their part, both on offense and defense. It's amazing when you think about it, but whoever invented baseball—and it wasn't Abner Doubleday—figured it out pretty well. It's ninety feet between bases, which is perfect. Anything else would be too long or too short. The same with the distance from the pitcher's mound to home plate. And each field is unique. Look at Fenway Park. The Green Monster is thirty feet high. Do you know why? Because Lansdowne Street is right behind left field, so they couldn't make the left-field line any longer, so they made the wall higher, and now it's a landmark. When people see it, they instantly know it's Fenway Park. You can't say that about most of the modern stadiums. Compare that to tennis. With the exception of Wimbledon and a couple of others, most tennis facilities are all alike. Forest Hills was a great place for the U.S. Open. Lots of charm. You can't say that about the tennis center where the Open is played now. That's one thing that makes golf unique, too. Every hole and every course is different. You can't get bored.

I know you have a great sense of history. . . .

It comes from growing older. I know I'm on the back nine of life, but I hope it's only about the twelfth hole.

But is that why golf and baseball appeal to you?

That's certainly a part of it. When the old Boston Garden was torn down and replaced, I made sure I got a piece of the old parquet floor the Celtics played on. I can understand the business reasons behind a new arena, but yes, there's a part of me that was nostalgic for the old Garden. But both games lend themselves to history. I just enjoy old courses more than new ones. I've played Bandon Dunes and it's a great course, but I don't enjoy it as much as I enjoy playing The Country Club in Brookline and knowing I'm playing the course where Francis Ouimet won the 1913 U.S. Open. You can't manufacture that unique sense of history, that special feel. The same for Old Head in Ireland. It's a wonderful course, but it's not the same as playing the classic old courses from the nineteenth century.

I know you enjoy playing with your kids. Did your dad get you started in the game?

I grew up in New York, but we used to play at the Hollywood Golf Club in Deal, New Jersey. My father was a very proper individual. He believed in the importance of etiquette and playing by the rules. There was a right way to play and everything else was wrong. The first year after I started learning the game, he wouldn't let me play. He insisted I just walk the course with him and watch him play. When I started to actually play, he didn't care how well I played. All he cared about was how I conducted myself on the course and how I treated other people. I see so many golfers today who don't know the etiquette and the rules.

Was your dad a good golfer?

He enjoyed the game but he wasn't a particularly great player, and he was a terrible putter, which I hope I didn't inherit from him. He could 3-putt from anywhere. But playing with my father provided a very important connection between us.

What about between you and your children?

Yes. It's interesting, because I play tennis with them, too, but it's a much different experience. The time we play is a lot shorter, and it's more competitive. One of my fondest memories was visiting my son, Teddy, in Milwaukee on his thirtieth birthday. We went to a par-3 course, and I beat him on the last hole. It was so much fun, and I saved the card. I treasure it. When I went through my divorce, it was a very difficult time. Teddy flew out from Milwaukee just to play golf with me. It meant so much to me. I played great, too. I was even par at Riviera.

Teddy and I have gone to Ireland and Scotland several times with my best friend and a couple of his kids. You can play until eight thirty or nine in the summer, so we play thirty-six a day. It's magical.

Do you have a favorite course over there?

I have so many that I love, but Tralee Golf Club in Ireland has a special charm for me. Everyone loves Royal

County Down and Portstewart and the other classics, but this is a jewel.

Why is it that so many parents and their children bond through golf?

Most children live in a perpendicular universe from their parents, but for the time you play golf together, they're stuck with you. It's just a great time to slow down, take a break from the world, laugh and enjoy the time together.

You live in a very competitive environment. Is that true when you play golf?

I shed most of my problems when I'm on the golf course. It's very hard to concentrate on golf and think about other things. Every round, for me, is about slowing down. That's why I enjoy it more when I walk. I can get into a rhythm. I don't go into a round with a lot of high expectations. I expect to make a certain number of pars.

Do you like to bet on your rounds?

No. Again, I have enough stress and pressure in my work life. I find that when I gamble, it changes the dynamic of the game.

Do you like playing with golfers who are better than you?

I do notice what other people are doing, but basically I like playing with people I enjoy being with and who help me relax. There's nothing worse than getting a half hour into a round and thinking, "Oh my god. I have to spend another four hours with this person."

If you could play in a dream foursome, whom would it include?

Jesus, Moses, and Mohammed.

If you could have been a professional golfer, who would you like to have been?

Besides you? Actually I've never enjoyed watching tournament golf as much as I enjoy playing the game. I admire people like Jack Nicklaus, Arnold Palmer, and Tiger, and I'm friends with Brad Faxon, but I've never been as absorbed by professional golf as I am by other sports.

What's your favorite golf movie?

I'm not sure I have a favorite movie, but my favorite scene is from *The Honeymooners.* Hoping for a promotion, Jackie Gleason has told his boss that he plays golf and now has just two days to prepare for a round with him. Gleason enlists his friend Art Carney's help in learning how to play. Carney, reading aloud from a golf instruction book, says, "The first thing you have to do is address the ball." Both guys have no idea what that means. After rereading the text, Carney says he thinks he now knows. Stepping up to the ball, he roars, "Hello, ball!" Everything about the scene is a classic.

Occasionally you have a round of golf when there seems to be an inevitability about playing well. Do you have that sense with a television series?

You have a sense when something is really special and when it's not going to work. With *The Cosby Show* we knew it was special right away. The key is not straying from what your intention was right from the beginning.

• • •

I've come to have a genuine respect and affection for Tom. He's a great role model in both golf and life. There's a great depth and breadth to the man. He's in a challenging business, but he's not a macho guy. He's a person who appreciates the poetry in golf, baseball, and life.

JERRY WEST

G ROWING UP in Los Angeles, I can't really say that I was a passionate basketball fan, but of course I knew who Jerry West was. You'd need to have lived on another planet not to. Not only was he the best player the L.A. Lakers had, he was one of the best players in the National Basketball Association. In fact, some people think he was the greatest guard in the history of the sport.

Jerry grew up in West Virginia, played for West Virginia University, and, after leading the United States team to a gold medal in the 1960 Olympics, he joined the Lakers, where he played for fourteen seasons. After he retired, he was named to the Naismith Memorial Hall of Fame and the NBA Hall of Fame. In addition, he was named one of the NBA's 50 Greatest Players and was a member of ten All-NBA First Teams, as well as thirteen All-Star Teams.

He coached the Lakers from 1976 to 1979 and then be-

AMY ALCOTT

came their general manager. In 2002, he became president
of basketball operations for the NBA's Memphis Grizzlies.
He was named the NBA Executive of the Year twice.

I got to know Jerry through golf, first at Riviera Country Club and later at Bel-Air Country Club. He is one of
the finest amateurs I've ever played with (and against;
we've had our share of money games over the years). He
has the physical skills, and he is as tough a competitor
as any I've ever run across. He absolutely hates losing. I
mean he really, really hates it.

We talked in the grill room at Bel-Air, and as our interview went on, I got to see a side of him I'd never seen before—
and came to understand what made him the consummate
competitor and professional.

. . .

*I understand that you took up golf almost by accident. Is
that true?*

Well, I didn't play as a kid, and might have never taken
up the game if I hadn't been given a set of clubs when I
joined the Lakers. I went over to a driving range on Lincoln
Boulevard [in Los Angeles] and just started hitting these
monstrous slices. I became fascinated by the golf swing and
the act of compressing the ball. It appealed to my curiosity.
I just wanted to figure out how the swing worked, and as a

competitor I wanted to improve. It just bothered me that I couldn't excel at a sport.

Things were a lot different then. The season wasn't as long and we had more spare time. Also, no one really cared that much about the Lakers in the early sixties. We were on the back pages of the sports section, and no one was making much money. Guys played because they just loved the game and the competition. I could go to the driving range and never be bothered.

Do you remember your first round?

It was at a public course over on Western Avenue. I shot a 99.

Does your basketball experience carry over to golf?

In some ways, but not in others. A lot of it is psychological rather than physical. A lot of it has to do with how you deal with pressure. Facing a shot or a putt under pressure is a lot like having a clutch shot from the corner at the buzzer. I always wanted the ball in that situation, and that carried over to golf.

In athletics, the person you're battling is yourself, not the other players. That's how you define yourself as an athlete and a competitor, and I think that's especially true in an individual sport like golf. In that sense, it carried over from basketball. I was always thinking about how I can make myself a better player and what I can do to help us win.

I had a wonderful career, that's true. But I never enjoyed the success that comes from winning championships. We went to the NBA finals nine times and won once. The worst experience I ever had in sports was being named the Most Valuable Player in the 1969 finals but losing to Boston. It was the worst feeling ever, ever, ever. Knowing I played better than everyone else and we still lost, that was horrible. It was the worst feeling in my life. Bill Russell came into our locker room after the game and just took my hand. He didn't say a word. He didn't have to. He knew exactly how I felt and I knew he knew. There is no satisfaction in sports unless you win. That's the ultimate thrill.

Is that desire to win what sets you and other great athletes apart?

It's part of it, but I sometimes think it's fate or something. It's almost like there's a halo around certain people, that the good Lord sprinkled a little extra gold dust on them. A great basketball, football, or hockey player sees the game differently. It's like they see things in slow motion. I always felt I could see what was *going* to happen, while 99.9 percent of the players only see what's happening. I've heard Wayne Gretzky say the same thing. I was never surprised by something someone did. Never. I think that's a gift. I don't think you can learn it.

And dealing with the pressure?

I never felt I was going to choke. I felt I was prepared and knew what I needed to do. I really never felt any pressure except to improve. That's what separates the great players from the others. They just love the competition. Jack Nicklaus is a great example of that. And there's a certain desire for perfection and willingness to do the work necessary to achieve it. I remember back when I could play golf pretty well that nothing would frustrate me more than making eighteen straight pars. It just killed me that if I could play well enough to do that, I should be able to make a couple of birdies. It really bothered me.

You retired as a player after fourteen seasons. Did you just get tired of it all or maybe get burned out?

Unless you've succeeded at the highest levels of a sport, people can't understand how much success takes out of you. You sit in the locker room before a game and you feel as though your body is electrically charged. I don't know any other way to explain it. And then you go out and play as hard and as long as you can. Eventually it takes a toll. In my case, it wasn't difficult to retire because I knew it was time. I used to sit in the locker room before a game and sweat would pour off my hands. Then one time we were about to go out on the floor for an exhibition game and my hands were completely dry. That's when I knew I didn't have it inside me anymore, and if I couldn't live up to my expectations, I wasn't going to play anymore. For me, it was never about the money. I've seen a lot of guys hang on too long in the NBA. To be honest, as much as I admire Arnold Palmer and Jack Nicklaus, I wish they had retired sooner.

Was it difficult for you to excel in a solitary sport like golf when you had been such a great team player?

Even though I played a team sport, I was very much a loner and narcissistic, and I think golf appealed to me for that reason. I have a very complex private side and I just felt I could immerse myself in the game. It's incredibly addictive. I like the fact that you can go out on the course by yourself. It can be very serene. I do think there's something very mysterious about the game. You never quite get it. I don't think anyone really does. I also like the fact that the game is never going to change fundamentally. Players will get bigger and stronger and the equipment will improve, but the core of the game will remain the same. In the end, I guess what I like about golf is that it is such a solitary game. One of my few regrets is that I didn't pursue the game when I retired. I was only thirty-five, which is when golfers are in their prime. I wonder how I could have done competing against the best players in the game.

How's your game today?

Age changes all of us, no matter how good an athlete you are. I'm mellower, but I still have the need to compete. As you get older you don't concentrate as well, which reflects in your score.

You said you admired Arnold Palmer and Jack Nicklaus. . . .

When I used to go to the L.A. Open, I would rarely go out on the course. I'd go to the practice range and watch the players. I was a pretty decent player, but when I'd watch Nicklaus, Trevino, Weiskopf, Watson, guys like that, I'd realize I wasn't even close. They are geniuses. I mean, the ball just sounded different when they hit it. What I also admired about guys like Nicklaus was that they handled themselves with such grace, win or lose. They accepted responsibility for their play, good or bad. They never complained. In golf, it's just you. It's not the caddy or the weather or anything else, and that appeals to me.

What do you think about Tiger Woods?

He's a unique athlete. There are players who can dominate their sport but he towers above everyone. No one is even close in terms of determination, skill, and courage. Sometime I'd like to see him tied with a few guys with four holes to play and have him make four straight pars. He'd still win because he's so intimidating that they'd make mistakes. I've never seen an athlete who is as intimidating as Tiger. People say he plays against Jack Nicklaus's record. That's wrong. He doesn't play against Jack. He doesn't play against the field. He doesn't play against the course. He plays against himself and his standards. He's constantly battling to define himself as a competitor and an athlete and that's why he's such a fantastic champion.

If you could play in a dream foursome, would he be part of it?

I don't know. I love to read, and two of the people I admire the most are Franklin Roosevelt and Winston Churchill, not only because of what they did but for their speeches. If you just read them you realize what a remarkable ability to communicate they had and how they used it to lead people. I guess I'd like to spend time with them and maybe Thomas Jefferson or any of the Founding Fathers. Our Constitution is the greatest document ever written.

What do you think your legacy is?

I could care less about my legacy. I never worried about people liking me and I don't take myself too seriously. People knew I went out there to compete. I put substance ahead of style, which is the complete opposite of our society today. I think writers, artists, and musicians leave legacies, not athletes. I had my day in the sun and I don't have any illusions. I like to think I was disciplined, educated, worked hard, and treated people with respect, and I'm comfortable with that.

. . .

Jerry West is a man with great natural talent, discipline, and razor-sharp focus who had a vision to be the best he could be, pursued his dream, and made it come true. He is also a man who seeks knowledge and enlightenment outside his career. That is part of his complex makeup and the side I most admire and can relate to in a big way, because very often the public sees only the athlete and doesn't know how multidimensional most of us are.

JACK WHITAKER

NEITHER OF MY PARENTS played golf, so my first real exposure to the game was almost by accident: one day I turned on the television and there was the *CBS Golf Classic,* a made-for-television series of matches played at the Firestone Country Club in Akron, Ohio. I was hooked almost from the beginning, in part because I thought so many of the players had such strange names—Kermit or Orville or Butch. For the longest time, I thought a lot of players were named "Pards," because players kept saying to each other, "Nice shot, pards."

Besides being fascinated by the golf, I loved watching and listening to Jack Whitaker, an announcer on the series. To me, he just looked like someone who should be out covering golf from exotic parts of the world. He was handsome, dressed beautifully (I loved the tweed caps he wore), and had the most wonderful voice. He was just so witty and urbane. I think he personified the "greatest generation" of television sports journalists, and I'm glad we got to visit over martinis every now and then.

Over the years, first with CBS and then with ABC, he covered golf, horse racing, the Olympics, and just about every major sporting event you could imagine. While he was wonderful at play-by-play, he became best known for his on-air essays, which were elegantly crafted, done from the heart, and usually summed up the event he had just covered. Nobody, before or since, has done them with more literacy or grace.

One of Jack's essays has a special meaning for me. When I won the 1991 Nabisco Dinah Shore for the third time, he was covering the tournament for ABC. He closed the broadcast with one of his stylish essays, saying, "Wow, what can you say, Amy had a walk in the sun this week with her wire-to-wire win here in the Coachella Valley. She may be no competition for Greg Louganis with her jump into the lake, but this young Southern California native with the Christmas-morning smile, great style, and aggressive play bodes well for the future of the LPGA." Jack's words are always poetic, and what he said meant so much to me. It brought tears to my eyes when I saw it on tape the next day. It still does today.

Jack is a native of Philadelphia, but for the last twenty years he's lived primarily in the Palm Springs area. I visited him in his Indian Wells home and we began by speaking about the early years of his career.

. . .

I got my start in Philadelphia doing sports on a local station. Four days after Labor Day in 1950, I met Frank Chirkinian [who would go on to become the legendary producer and director of CBS's golf coverage, as well as other sports], and we cut our teeth together in what was a very young business. Frank always loved golf, and when he was directing my show he came up with the idea of doing a fifteen-minute program each Wednesday with George Fazio, who was one of the top professionals in the area. People loved it. I've never received as much mail as I received for that program.

Golf was just taking off at the time. Ben Hogan was the big story. In the post–World War II years, people had more spare time and a little extra money, so golf enjoyed a boom of sorts. I had taken up the game in 1948, playing with my wife's clubs. I thought golf was pretty exciting at the time. Little did I know what heartache awaited me. As Bernard Darwin wrote, "Golf is not a funeral, although both can be sad affairs."

I asked him if golf was his favorite sport.

Baseball was my first love and still is, really. Back in those days we had the A's and the Phillies. But in those days, I covered all the sports. We were sort of jacks of all trades. But I came to love golf. I would say it's my favorite sport to cover, followed by horse racing. I had pretty impressive events to cover the first time out in both sports. The first golf tournament I ever broadcast was the 1960 PGA Championship at Aronimink, which Gary Player won. My first horse race was a Kentucky Derby. Both sports attract intelligent writers because of the people involved. There are so many interesting characters in both sports that they are naturals for journalists.

When I asked him if he considered himself a journalist, he paused to consider his answer.

That's hard to say. I never went to journalism school, but I read a lot and I made a point of keeping up with my contacts in the sports I covered. I'm not sure you can do that today, because athletes don't really trust the press anymore, and with good reason in some cases. But back then we were friends. There was a lot less money and so there was a lot less pressure. I try to look at what I do as a craft more than an art. It's kind of frightening and exciting to be in a situation where you have a limited amount of time to pull all the information together and then present it in a graceful way while the seconds are ticking off your mental clock. It's work, but when you pull it off, you can allow yourself the luxury of thinking, "My God, I hit that one pretty well."

We talked about how he got started doing his essays.

I always loved writing and used to do the essays on my local show in Philadelphia. When I came to CBS, I did the second Super Bowl. I asked the director, Tony Verna, who was a Philadelphia guy, if I could do a ninety-second essay summing up the game. He gave me a shot and it took off from there.

Anyone who was around professional golf from the mid-1960s through 1996, when Frank Chirkinian retired from CBS, knew that their broadcast team was like a family—and sometimes an unruly family. But most people considered them the best in the business. Among others, the team included Jack, Ken Venturi, Pat Summerall, Ben Wright, Frank Gleiber, and Jim Nantz. Jack spoke about those days, as well as how the business has changed since then.

Well, first of all, you have to go back to Frank [Chirkinian]. He wasn't called the Ayatollah for nothing. He ran a tight ship but he got the best out of everyone. And we were like a family. We had dinner together every night. We played golf together. We stayed in touch in the off-season. We were there for each other in the good times and bad times. There was very little jealousy. It was a more romantic era of broadcasting. When I went to ABC in 1982, it was a different atmosphere. Rossie (Bob Rosburg), Dave Marr, and I would have dinner together but everyone else seemed to go their own way.

Today, everyone seems to be trying to get their own shtick. That's fine. But with Frank it was more of an ensemble. Everyone had a role to play. Now, I'm not so sure it works as well. I watch CBS golf and I think I'm listening to the BBC. But times change and you can't stay rooted in the past. When Gary McCord joined CBS, people criticized him, but he found a way to stand out and he still got his knowledge of the game across. He probably went over the line with his "bikini wax" comments about Augusta's greens. I wouldn't have said that, but it did get his point across.

His mention of Gary McCord, who was banned from Augusta National for his comments, led me to ask about Augusta's banishment of him following the 1966 Masters.

Jack had just won a Monday playoff with Tommy Jacobs and Gay Brewer. We absolutely had to be off the air right at seven o'clock for the [CBS] *Evening News* with Walter Cronkite. I had thirty seconds to sum everything up. The gallery had crushed in around the eighteenth green, which is what we were showing, and I said something about it being a "mob scene." Clifford Roberts [the chairman of Augusta National] claimed I called their patrons a mob, which wasn't what I said. Anyway, I just don't think they liked my work and used it as an excuse to get rid of me. The funny thing was, about four or five years later I was at the Masters and

Frank asked me to fill in for one of his announcers. I was delighted, but first we had to go clear it with Cliff Roberts. My God, you'd think nothing had ever happened. He welcomed me back with open arms.

Jack turned eighty-three in May 2007, and I asked if he had any regrets about his career.

Not really. Sometimes I think what I did wasn't very important in the great scheme of things. I remember doing a Super Bowl one year and there was a crisis and it looked like we and the Russians were going to blow up the world. I remember wondering why I was so concerned about a football game at that particular moment. Another time I was watching Alexander Haig, who grew up near me in Philadelphia, testify before the Senate in his confirmation process to become secretary of state. I wondered why him and not me. If I had one wish, it would have been to address a joint session of Congress. I'm not sure what I would have said, but I would have enjoyed it. Do I wish I had discovered a cure for cancer? Sure. But in the end, I enjoyed what I did and had a wonderful life. I brought enjoyment to people and I think my kids are proud of me. Besides, after a round of golf, I have a wealth of stories I can share with my friends over a couple of drinks, with my face aglow from the sun and my heart happy with the joy of friendship. It can't get better than that.

. . .

Jack Whitaker's life teaches us to find something we love and shape it and polish it until we call it our own. That's what he did with his essays. There are hundreds, maybe thousands, of people who announce sports events, but precious few who dare to try to follow in Jack's footsteps, in part because his incomparable instincts and preparation were unique.

In the early days of the British Open, the winner received the Champion's Belt. When Young Tom Morris won his third straight Open championship in 1870, he retired the belt, and no championship was held the following year.

When it comes to writing and presenting sports essays and commentary on television, Jack Whitaker retired the belt. I'm glad to say he's been both a mentor and a dear friend over the years.

JOHN WILLIAMS

I'VE ALWAYS CONSIDERED GOLF as much an artistic activity as an athletic one, which may be one reason why I
have so much respect and admiration for my friend John
Williams, the brilliant composer, conductor, and musician.
His works are among the most familiar of anyone composing today. Most people know John best for the scores
he has written for—among many other films—*Jaws, Star
Wars, Close Encounters of the Third Kind, Superman, Raid-
ers of the Lost Ark, E.T., Schindler's List, Saving Private
Ryan, Memories of a Geisha,* and *Harry Potter and the Sor-
cerer's Stone.* He has won five Academy Awards, eighteen
Grammys, three Golden Globes, four Emmys, and three
BAFTA Awards.

For many years John was the principal conductor of the
Boston Pops Orchestra, a civic treasure that is nearly as
beloved as the Red Sox (and believe me, that's saying something). He is also an artist-in-residence at the Tanglewood

Festival in Lenox, Massachusetts, the summer home of the Boston Symphony Orchestra.

John and I met several years ago at Bel-Air Country Club, where both of us are members. He refers to our late-afternoon rounds of golf together there as "walks" because for him, the sheer pleasure of walking a beautiful golf course is at least as important as the golf itself. We began our conversation with his poignant story about how he came to take up the game.

. . .

About thirty years ago, when I was in my forties, my wife passed away. I took her death very hard and would spend time moping around at the Twentieth Century-Fox studio. A couple of older colleagues suggested I take up golf. I had caddied a little bit as a youngster growing up in New York, but never took it very seriously, and the thought of playing a game where grown men wore plaid pants wasn't very appealing. I joined Bel-Air thinking I would just play tennis, but when I discovered the incredible privilege of simply walking around this beautiful preserve—and that's really what a golf course is—I found it intoxicating and the game became an addiction.

I know from our conversations over the years that you've developed an almost spiritual feeling about the game.

Well, I'm a tree lover in the true sense of the word. I feel the sanctity of the trees and the grass enriching. I think they touch us as part of our psychic makeup. Being out on a beautiful golf course gives me a deep connection with nature. Then, of course, you add a stick and a ball and it presents a challenge. I never get bored with the game. I also think that golf has a certain integrity and elegance. There's an atmosphere of politeness that appeals to me. Our lives are like moving from one traffic jam to the next and then suddenly we have this great privilege of walking around this place that is like a royal deer park in Denmark. It is quite precious. For me, golf is a game of respite and, often, seclusion. And of course it filled a void in my life after my wife died. Now I play with my daughter, which I cherish. It has given us the greatest connection. It's something we can do together.

I also like golf because you can never master it. No one can. It never gives you everything. It's given you a lot but it always holds something back. You can win a golf tournament but you can always look back and see something you could have done better. There are a lot more perfect performances in music than in golf. The game also puts you in touch with your own limitations. It's a great leveler and it teaches you the importance of keeping your sense of humor.

But the real beauty of the game is that every so often, maybe once in a hundred times, even a high-handicapper can hit a Tiger Woods shot. It's that perfect shot that brings you back. It's that taste of what greatness is like. What else in life can give you that?

Have you ever had a hole in one?

Two, both here at Bel-Air, but they weren't perfect shots. They weren't even very good shots. I hit them both thin and they somehow managed to run into the hole.

Your work as a composer is very solitary. Does golf appeal to you because you can be with other people?

No, I wouldn't say that's one of its appeals. When I'm composing I need quiet, and one of the things about golf is the serenity that being on the course provides. I like playing with a friend but foursomes are very hard for me.

Do you compose when you're on the course?

I don't develop themes as much as I solve musical problems. I find that the oxygen level increases, and that helps clarify my thinking.

Do you find any similarities between music and golf?

In some respects, yes. There's a difference between composing and performing. Instrumental technique, for example, is very similar to golf. There's an old saying: if a pianist misses a day of practice, he knows; if he misses two days, the audience knows; and if he misses three days, the critics know. It's a matter of muscle memory in both playing an instrument and playing golf. I also think that a person who takes up an instrument or learns golf when they are young has a much greater chance of success. I don't know any truly accomplished pianist who took up playing after the age of fourteen. Also, you can't think about what your hands are doing when you're playing the piano and I don't think you can when you're hitting a golf shot.

Do you think you can learn to be a great pianist or is it really a gift?

Again, there are similarities. You can become technically proficient, but can you exhibit genius? Probably not. Hard work will only get you so far and the same is true in golf. Ninety-nine percent of all golfers could take lessons from the best professional and work extremely hard, but are they going to become a Tiger Woods or an Amy Alcott? No.

What about the role discipline plays?

In my case, it was very important. My father was an accomplished musician and he was kind of a dictatorial guy—not in the sense that he was abusive, but he knew the challenges I'd face and wanted me to be prepared for them. For example, I couldn't go out and play baseball until I had practiced the piano. In my case, it worked. I tried the same approach with my kids but it didn't work. It's a generational thing. I was either compliant towards my father or interested enough in the piano to do the necessary work. I imagine it's the same thing in golf. You only get out what you're willing to put in.

What about the role rhythm plays in the golf swing?

Certainly there's a rhythmic component to all athletics. For that matter, a piano concerto can be an athletic event. But you can see it in the golf swing. Players like Lee Trevino and Jim Furyk have great variations in their technique but they have wonderful rhythm. What interests me is the mental mechanics. What causes a player to get out of rhythm, both in their swing and in their thinking?

Part of the difficulty in golf is that you have so much time between shots. It allows negative thoughts to creep into your head. That's why I think you play your best golf when you're not thinking. You want to just get in a zone.

Yes, that's true. We get in our own way. Thinking is an interruption when you're conducting. It takes you out of the zone where you need to be. Also, another factor is that in golf, your muscles get a chance to cool down between swings. In conducting, that doesn't happen.

Any other similarities that come to mind?

When I'm composing a film score, I look at it as a challenge. I'm being asked to use all my knowledge and experience to solve the challenges and problems it presents. It's like the time [violinist] Isaac Stern was asked which was his favorite violin concerto. "The one I'm performing," he said. Then he was asked which was the most difficult. His answer was the same: "The one I'm performing." As a golfer, when you go to a U.S. Open, you're being asked to use all your skill and knowledge and experience to figure out the challenge the course is presenting you. In both cases, there are always banana peels out there. You can always slip.

Is writing film scores a unique challenge?

Film offers a tremendous canvas to work on, one that Mozart and Wagner didn't have. Imagine if Wagner wrote film scores? He'd own the studio. Plus, the stage is so much bigger. If I conduct a concert, twenty-five hundred people will experience it. When I write a score for a Steven Spielberg movie, billions of people hear it. All communication today is globalization.

Toward the end of my Tour days, I just became bored with golf. Do you ever get bored with music?

I don't think you were bored with golf. You were tired of the Tour and the traveling. That's an enormous difference. Senior musicians may retire from performing but they haven't lost their love for music. In fact, I would argue that as you grow older, your love for music grows. I think the same is true in golf. When you're ninety, you'll still be out there chipping and putting. The love affair grows deeper and deeper. I think it's very spiritual.

Would you have rather been Ben Hogan or Ted Williams? I mean, would you have rather played an individual sport or a team sport?

It's easier for me to be a conductor than to play in an orchestra. I got bored with that. I remember coming home after performing *West Side Story* and telling my wife I was finished performing. I just couldn't do it anymore. Hogan or Williams? I so treasure the solace I get from walking a golf course I'd go with Hogan. I couldn't get that at Fenway Park.

If you could play with any three people, who would they be?

That's a good question. I love playing with my daughter. Maybe Bill Clinton, because I so respect and admire him. Emily Dickinson would be interesting. And Beethoven. He eventually became deaf, so he wouldn't be able to hear the sound of a bad shot.

Finally, I want to ask you if you have a favorite composition.

They're all so different. I always come away thinking I wish I could have done it better, but occasionally things get beyond your control, just like in golf. I will say that *Close Encounters of the Third Kind* is special because it became alive. It was organic. Again, like in golf, you know when something is really good.

.   .   .

John Williams has a deep appreciation of nature. It is central to his character. One day he quoted verse from Edward Elgar, the British composer, to me: "Are the trees singing my song or am I singing theirs?" The more I thought about that, the more I realized that golf gives us a chance to hear nature speaking to us . . . if we will only listen.

ACKNOWLEDGMENTS

FIRST, I'D LIKE to thank Don Wade for helping me write this book. We've been friends for thirty years, and this is the second book we've collaborated on. It was a lot of fun working together and renewing what has been a long and remarkable friendship.

My thanks simply to the game of golf and the LPGA Tour, with its rich history and world-class competitors, which gave me an arena to showcase my talent and to walk a memorable path. Golf is definitely the gift that keeps on giving.

I also want to thank my friend and business adviser, Linda Giaciolli, and my friend Susan Hunt, who assisted in the interview process. Also, my brother Bruce, whose support has been unwavering. The same is true for Judith Curr, the publisher of Atria Books, and Nick Simonds, my editor at Atria, for their insights and belief in *The Leaderboard*. I'd also like to thank my literary agent, Amy Rennert, for her thoughtful advice throughout the entire process.

Also, I can't overlook my dogs, Little B, the Scottie, and Juliet, the Lakie.

I want to note that another source of encouragement was President Bill Clinton. He and I chatted when he was writing *My Life* and he urged me to write this book, saying, "Girl, just do it. We all have at least one book inside of us."

Finally, I'd like to thank all my friends who agreed to be included in this book. Their interest in *The Leaderboard* means a lot to me. Their friendship means much more.

—*Amy Alcott*